MICHAEL C. GI

MW01165989

THE DOPELESS HOPE FIEND

$2\frac{2}{75}$

7^{50}
22
15^{00}
150^{00}
185^{00}

THE DOPELESS HOPE FIEND

VETERAN POLICE OFFICER BECOMES HOMELESS DRUG ADDICT BEFORE FINDING REDEMPTION AFTER NEAR DEATH EXPERIENCE

MICHAEL CHARLES GIVENS

FIRST EDITION

GREEN SHAWL PUBLISHERS

THE DOPELESS HOPE FIEND

Veteran police officer becomes homeless drug addict before finding redemption after near death experience by Michael C. Givens

Green Shawl

Publishers

Richmond, CA.

http://www.thedopelesshopefiend.com

Unattributed quotations are by Michael Charles Givens

ISBN 978-0-615-30767-1

PCN pfs65350

First edition 2009   Printed in the United Stated of America

The Dopeless Hope fiend depicts the lessons learned and the life experiences of the author. The names and qualities of all other characters in this publication have been changes in the interest of their protection. Similarities to many characters to people in real life are strictly coincidental.

ACKNOWLEDGEMENTS

First and foremost, I would like to praise and give thanks to God who is truly the light of my life. You twice preserved my life when I was near death. Without you I would be nothing nor have anything. I sincerely believe that you have guided my fingers along my keyboard that fed my computer the words that are expressed in this book.

God sometimes sends angels. The one he has sent to me was in the form of my mother, Shirley Croft. You had maintained a constant vigil at the bedside that some thought would be my death bed and prayed me back to health. You are always there when I need you. I love you.

I would also like to recognize my siblings, Larry, Matthew, and Lamarah and my step-dad Bill Croft. You four prayed for me when I was in my mess and loved me from a distance. I love you all.

The prayer warriors at The Market Street Seven Day Adventist Church has reserved a special place in my heart.

My late sponsor and confidant Ralph R. Thanks for saving my life. May you rest in peace.

To my friend and business associate Elizabeth Williams. Thank you for your generosity in funding this project. Your kindness will never be overlooked.

My son Michael Jr. and my daughter Mila. I have been very unfair to you both. I was not there for you during the most important years of your lives and it is my loss that I have not gotten to know you better. I offer no excuses. I do love you both and I pray for you everyday. Please forgive me.

CONTENTS

SELDOMLY HAVE WE SEEN A PERSON
FAIL WHO HAS THOROUGHLY
FOLLOWED OUR PATH

Alcoholics Anonymous

PREFACE-NOTE FROM THE AUTHOR
TO THE <u>NON-SOBER</u> ADDICT

There was once an addict that was stuck in a deep hole. A doctor came along. The addict explained his situation to the doctor and the doctor wrote out a prescription, threw it down to the addict then walked away. Shortly thereafter, a priest walked by. When the addict asked the priest for help, the priest wrote out a prayer, threw it down to the addict and walked away. A recovering addict soon came along and after hearing of the addict's plight, the recovering addict jumped into the hole with the addict. The addict said, "What are you doing? Now we're both stuck. We'll never get out of here alive." The recovering addict then said, "It's OK. I've been down here before and I know the way out. Follow me."

I wrote "The Dopeless Hope Fiend" for the purpose of sharing my experience, strength, faith and hope so that another addict may find the way out of the deep hole of addiction in which we dwell.

My story is no different from the story of any other addict that's been down in that hole. We tried tunneling out, climbing out, some of us even tried to fly out of the hole, but we found that the walls were too dense to tunnel; they were too slippery to climb and no matter how hard we flapped our arms we failed to rise after hitting bottom.

Friends and family members tried to 'fix" us and many of us stopped drinking and doping for a time. We followed their prescriptions as <u>we</u> attempted to answer their prayers. But before long we realized that they were not familiar enough with the ailment to write the proper prescription and only GOD can answer prayers.

Most of us became way too comfortable sitting in that hole and we made the hole our home. We decorated the hole with artwork, furniture and even obtained cable TV for the hole until we discovered that the longer we stayed in the hole, the deeper became our bottom.

Out of desperation <u>we asked for help</u> and God sent angels that jumped into the hole with us. Angels that showed us the way out of the hole.

The angels showed us the path to recovery. Some of us thought that the path was straight and narrow but we were wrong.

We were confident that we could bear the winding turns on this path. And because we ignored the road map, we fell into one of the other holes that exist along this path.

We were rescued yet again. Though this time we used the road map so to avoid becoming stuck in one of the other holes that litter this path.

Among the greatest of the gifts that we were given is the gift of hope. Hope is the reason that we get out of bed in the morning. It gives us the motivation to face any task with confidence and vigor.

Faith cannot exist without hope. Faith allows us to walk this path without the fear of falling into another hole. Just for today

HOPE IS AN EXTENTION OF OUR FAITH THAT GOD WILL FULFILL HIS PROMISES

We see things very differently now. The hole offered a very narrow view of the world outside of it. Now that we are out, we can see to the horizon in all directions.

As the days passed and we became more and more familiar with the path, we see other addicts that are stuck in the same deep holes that we were in. We jump in and show them the way out and they are grateful.

Soon, they are jumping in the holes in order to guide their fellows and this wonderful chain continues.

We find it important to be patient with ourselves. We didn't become addicts in one day, one week, or one month. It took many years of practice and training to perfect the art of being a dope fiend.

RECOVERY IS NOT AN EVENT. IT IS A PROCESS.

If you think that you may be an addict and that you are ready to get unstuck and find your way out of that hole, I invite you to walk along this path with me. If you need to talk, call me. I'm ready to jump in.

Mike G.(510)860-7736

PREFACE-NOTE FROM THE AUTHOR
TO THE <u>SOBER</u> ADDICT

Y ou possess something that is valuable and powerful. It is more valuable than gold. In the whole world, there is nothing that can even come close to it's worth to certain segments of our society. Many will die horrible deaths or suffer great loss for lacking it.

It is not to be hoarded or put upon a shelf for later use; nor is it meant to be shamelessly used as a means to control others. Though it is priceless, it cannot be bought or sold. It must be given away.

WE KEEP WHAT WE HAVE BY GIVING
IT AWAY

Narcotics Anonymous

That thing of which I speak is your experience, strength and hope.We are the culmination of all of our experiences. Our experiences are who we are. So as a consequence, we are required to give ourselves away.

Somewhere along the way, <u>you</u> did something that too few addicts do. You "got it". You got the fact that you do not have to put mind and mood altering substances into your body to feel good or to avoid feeling bad. You got the fact that life is a spectacular event without the assistance of alcohol or drugs. That's a gift from GOD that is better than gold. Nothing could be more valuable to life.

It is a gift that must be given after it is received. There is no greater gift that we can bestow upon to another addict than the benefit of our experience, strength and hope.

The blessing of this thing that we call recovery is that we get to share it with those who need it.

In this book you will meet a wise and kind man whose name is Ralph. When I was in my mess, Ralph would always say, "Helping other addicts keeps me sober."

Ralph, I get it!

I WAS A HOPELESS DOPE FIEND. I BECAME A DOPELESS HOPE FIEND.

THIS IS MY STORY!

DOPE-FIEND-A person that exhibits an unusually strong desire for alcohol or drugs. He is a morally deprived character, driven by self serving compulsions and bent on manipulating and systematically relieving you of everything that you have.

Mike Givens

1

THE AWAKENING

APRIL 15, 2008

"**M**r. Givens... Mr. Givens. Everything is alright. You have had open heart surgery. You can't talk because there is a breathing tube in your throat. Please try to relax," was the first thing that I remember hearing as I awakened in a foggy haze in this strange environment. As my vision cleared, I noticed the smiling young nurse speaking with a heavy West African accent standing over me as I laid on a hospital bed in the intensive care ward at Summit Hospital.

"The doctor will come by later to remove your breathing tube. You are a very lucky man. Most people that undergo the type of surgery you underwent don't survive. You have visitors here to see you."

I turned my head as much as I could toward the door to see my mother enter the room. I later learned that she had maintained a constant vigil at my bedside during the three weeks that I was in a coma.

She was flanked by my older brother, Larry, who had taken leave from his job and had flown here to Oakland, California from his home in Canada out of concern for my well being. My muscle bound younger brother Matthew and my gorgeous younger sister Lamarah were not far behind.

I could see the concern on their faces and was touched by their outpouring of love and affection.

I have no recollection of the series of events that led to my hospitalization. The last thing that I remembered doing was walking hard pavement, pulling a heavy grocery cart collecting bottles and cans for recycling.

Unfortunately, I clearly recall how I arrived at such a low point in my life.

My decision to abuse crack cocaine had caused me to loose everyone in my life and everything that I owned many times over. And my untreated, out of control hypertension combined with heavy drug use twice nearly cost me my life.

As I laid on that hospital bed encumbered by the glare of bright overhead lights, I thought about the thirteen years I wasted abusing drugs.

I also considered the life that I had abandoned. My ten years as a veteran police officer for the city of Oakland California, two marriages, two wonderful children, owner of a successful business, and a life that some folks my age would envy.

I gave it all up for the opportunity to become a homeless drug addict.

I wrote this book for the purpose of sharing my experiences, strength, faith and hope so that another addict will find a reason and means to get sober or that a sober addict will find the will and desire to remain sober for just one more day.

HOPE IS THAT THING THAT GIVES STRENGTH DIRECTION

.

Believe me, it is possible. And the rewards are great. I had forgotten how amazingly fantastic it felt being high without having mind and mood altering chemicals in my body.

Today, meeting and talking to people places me on an social high. Being with family and love ones stimulates that part of my brain that causes me to be high. I get high every time someone tells me that they have read something that I have written and that it has improved his or her life in some way. That is the grand slam of highs to me.

RECOVERY IS SIMPLE, BUT IT AIN'T EASY.

Alcoholics Anonymous

Once we admit to ourselves that we have a problem, then convince ourselves that we want to change, we have taken a most important step.

We merely have to decide that change is the most important thing in our lives.

The first thing that we have to do is decide that we no longer want to continue wasting the remainder of our lives chasing something that does not exist.

The second thing we have to do is to decide that we are worth much more than we have become.

A decision is a powerful thing. Every great thing that has ever been accomplished by any person was preceded by a decision to perform the wonderful thing. Dreams and aspirations are good, but if we don't decide to take action, those dreams are eventually forgotten. Those aspirations disappear.

Our great president, Barack Obama, once dreamed of some day becoming President of the United States. I am sure that some of his acquaintances thought that he had lost his mind. After all, he is black in a majority white country, he had little experience and he has a funny sounding name.

But Mr. Obama knew that he was worth more than the sum of all his parts. He broadened his vision and dreamed of the possibilities.

Sometime during the course of his dreaming, he decided that he would run for president. The rest is history.

The point is that if President Obama had not taken that fraction of a second to make that decision, he would probably still be the Senator from Illinois. Or perhaps even the community organizer from Chicago.

Imagine what would have happened if he had only dreamed and not decided to take action. In this case, President Osama's split second decision changed history.

NOTHING CHANGES IF NOTHING CHANGES

Alcoholics Anonymous

If there is something in our lives that needs to be changed for the good, we only have two choices. Do nothing and continue down the same old path of destruction and despair or decide to change our lives for good and reap the benefits of that decision.

I can guarantee that nothing is going to change for the better if we don't <u>decide</u> to change it.

We can also make history and the benefit of that decision could last for the rest of our lives. So let's take a second right now and decide to make history.

Turn the page. There's someone I'd like you to meet

WE ARE NOT BAD, GETTING GOOD,

WE ARE SICK, GETTING BETTER!

2

OAKLAND'S FINEST

JANUARY 23, 1982

I was asleep when I felt a gentle nudge and a kiss on the top of my bald head.

"Mike, wake up. You don't want to be late on your first day of your new job, do you?"

I woke to the aroma of freshly brewed coffee and to the sight of my beautiful wife of four months, Denise.

After showering I was met at the kitchen table in our small studio apartment by eggs, beef sausage, hash browns, toast, coffee and orange juice. Denise was already dressed for work and sat beside me at the table.

"Mike, are you excited about your first job since moving to California".

"Yes I am. It's been six months since I've worked. Ever since I left my job in New Orleans to move here in order to marry you. This job comes just in time. Between now and September, when the baby's due we can save some money."

"I know that you will do well".

"I hope so". Denise gently kissed my bald head again and I left for work.

I think that there was something about my head that turned her on. She was always grabbing, rubbing, slapping or kissing it. I don't think that she would have married me if I had hair.

When I arrived at my new employer, Bank of Oakland, I was introduced to the branch manager Sam Roberson. He insisted that I call him Sam. I was surprised that he was such a casual and informal person.

I had always envisioned bankers as being uptight and conservative. Sam introduced me to my immediate supervisor, Mrs. Jones, who was uptight and conservative. She insisted that I called her Mrs. Jones.

Mrs. Jones introduced me to Charlene who would train me for my position as a teller.

That morning, an armored truck had delivered a load of money. Charlene and I had the job of counting it to verify that all of the cash was there. I had never seen so much money in my life. My fingers were cramped by the time we finished.

Charlene introduced me to another teller whose name was John. John was a police officer with the City of

Oakland who was hired by the bank to work under cover as a teller to discourage robberies at this branch.

John and I had become good friends. Denise and John's wife Vanessa also became friends and in the ensuing months the four of us frequently met for social events .

John had tried on several occasions to convince me to join the Oakland police department, though I had no interest in becoming a police officer.

John and I were once at a pizza joint when he once again brought up the subject.

"Mike, the department is always looking for intelligent brothers like you and they are hiring right now. I'll bring you an application."

"Man, I told you that I'm not interested in becoming a cop. And besides, I'm twenty-one years old. I'm too young."

"No you are not. You are just the right age and you have a good head on your shoulders."

John thought for a while then turned toward me and said.

"I'll tell you what. This is what I'll do. I will bring you an application. After you submit it and go through the process, test and interviews, if you are not hired I will pay you one hundred fifty dollars cash. If you are hired, you pay me one hundred fifty dollars cash."

I thought about John's not so well thought through plan . If I were to intentionally screw up the interview for the purpose of collecting the one hundred fifty dollars, John would be none the wiser. Yeah, that's my plan. I turned to John and said, "It's a deal".

Faithfully, the next day, John arrived at the bank with the application which took me an entire two days to complete. The application packet was an inch thick.

After completing the application, I gave it back to John for submission. Two days later, I received a phone call from a Lt. Wilson who informed me that he would be conducting my background investigation and that I had been scheduled for a physical agility test that following day. He told me that I was highly recommended by John.

The physical agility test was a breeze. It included running one hundred feet, scaling a ten foot wall and walking an elevated beam.

The background investigation took six weeks. Lt. Wilson contacted all my relatives and everyone I knew, including my high school teachers in New Orleans.

I was not surprised that the worst thing that they discovered was that I was late for a college class once.

It had never occurred to me during the entire process that I would someday be a police officer. I was just going through this process to collect on the bet that John and I had made.

John had warned me about the final interview. He said that there would be four or five sergeants and lieutenants seated at a table and I would be seated in a chair in the middle of that room and that I would be bombarded with questions and placed in hypothetical police situations to test my judgment and response abilities.

This was finally my opportunity to sabotage my chances to get this job. I considered wearing jeans with holes in them and not showering but that would have been too obvious, so I dressed neatly and made my way downtown to the Police Administration Building.

The fact that I did not want the job probably accounted for the fact that I was so relaxed and gave such glib answers to their questions. I left the police administration building confident in the fact that I had blown the interview.

I was greeted at home by a wife with arms folded and a cold shoulder. Denise was never warm to the fact that she would be married to a police officer. She thought that the job was too dangerous.

"How was your interview?"

"Not good. I think I blew it."

"Good. Dinner is in the oven."

SEPTEMBER 20, 1982

I was sound asleep when I felt soft hands caressing my bald dome. There was a smile on my face even before I opened my eyes. I turned and softly kissed my wife who was now nearly nine months pregnant. She had been on maternity leave from her job for the past two weeks.

"Mike, you are going to be late if you don't get going. I'll make coffee".

"That's OK; you can rest. I'll stop at the coffee shop on the way to the bank."

It was 7:45Am. I had to get dressed and drive across town and be at the bank by 8:15AM.

I kissed Denise goodbye and as I walked out of the door I heard the phone ring. As I opened the car door, I heard Denise call out to me.

"Mike, you have an important phone call."

I ran to my porch where Denise was standing and took the phone from her.

"Hello"

"Hi Mike, I'm Sgt. Wayne with the Oakland Police Department. I am happy to inform you that you have been hired onto the department. You are scheduled to start the academy on September 27 at 8:00AM. Do you accept the position?"

I just stood there in complete shock for a few moments.

"Hello, Mike. Are you there?"

"Yea, I'm here and I accept."

Why in the hell did I say that? Never in my wildest dreams had I ever thought that I would be a cop. My first thought was, "Dam, now I have to pay John one hundred fifty dollars". I turned to Denise and told her the news.

"You're not going to accept that job are you? It's too dangerous. I'm too young to be a widow."

"I don't know. I told you that I only applied for the job to collect on that bet with John. I didn't actually think that they were going to hire me. We'll talk about it later. I 'm late for work."

I was so preoccupied on my drive to work that I passed my exit on Highway 80. For the first time in my life I was seriously considering being a cop. Police officers make good money and we needed it for the baby that was due any second. Not to mention the medical insurance and other benefits. My mind was made.

I was met at the door of the bank by John. He had a smirk on his face and his hand was extended as if he was pan handling. Apparently he had advance information that I had gotten the job.

"What's up John, are you looking for a handout?"

"Yes. A one hundred fifty dollars handout. Spare change is OK."

"Unless you will accept a third party, post dated, out of state check you will have to wait until I get my first check from the city."

I entered the bank and saw Sam sitting at his desk. I walked over to him and notified him of my decision to accept a position with the police department. He was happy for me and said that he understood why I was unable to give two weeks notice. I could only hope that

Denise would eventually come around and share my enthusiasm.

The drive home after work seemed to take forever. Denise was pretty upset when I left home that morning. She was raised in the hood in East Oakland and had a very low image of cops. Her older brother had been beaten badly and arrested by two Oakland cops on trumped up charges that were later dismissed. She also thought that the job would change me or that I would get hurt.

I stopped along the way and bought a bouquet of flowers and Chinese food from Denise's favorite restaurant.

When I pulled up in front of my home, I saw Denise sitting on the porch waiting for me. She managed to get up and waddle toward me encumbered by a very large belly.

"Mike, I just wanted to apologize for my attitude this morning. I just love you so much and I don't want to see you get hurt. But I trust your judgment and I am willing to go along with whatever you think is best for our family. Have you decided whether or not you're going to take the job?"

"I decided to accept. I don't want you to worry about me. After one year on the job, we'll talk. And if we determine that the job is too dangerous, I'll do something else with my life. OK?"

"That works for me. I love you very much, but I can't eat this food. It'll come up just as fast as it goes down. I don't think the baby likes Chinese."

"I figured as much. I will eat it for you then tell you what it tastes like."

"That's very kind of you. "

"No sacrifice is too great for my baby."

SEPTEMBER 27, 1982

It's 3:23 AM and I hadn't slept all night. The fact that I was to take my place in the Oakland Police Academy today was the cause of great apprehension and anxiety. This had been the longest night in my life. Time seem to have stood still as I stared at the digital alarm clock on the antique night stand next to the bed.

I finally dozed off about 4:30AM only to be awakened at 4:55AM by Denise.

"Mike, wake up. My water broke."

Being a veteran of Lamaze class, I knew exactly what to do. I immediately jumped out of bed and fell flat on my face. I was such a nervous wreck that I put my pants on, then discovered that they were on backwards.

Denise on the other hand was the picture of calm and cool. I helped her up, helped her to dress, and slowly helped her into the car. Once at the hospital Denise went into labor.

Because of all this excitement I completely forgot that I was suppose to start the academy that day. I called the patrol desk and told the officer that I had to miss my first day at work.

I felt a little guilty about calling in on my first day but they were very understanding.

At 11:52 AM, Michael C. Givens Jr. was born. He was a burley ten pounds six ounces. His bulk accounted for Denise's painful delivery which ended in a cesarean.

Mike Jr. had a big round melon shaped head and hazel colored eyes and was the most beautiful baby I had ever seen.

He was less than two minutes old when the nurse placed him in my arms. I thought that it was unusual that his eyes were open.

He looked at me when I spoke, as if he recognized my voice and he smiled. The nurse said that babies that young are incapable of smiling. She said that he probably just had a little gas. She was wrong. I know a smile when I see one.

The next day was my first day at the police academy. I was given two pairs of sweats with the Oakland Police logo printed on them, and then I and the entire class of forty-two recruits as a part of our physical conditioning, ran a mile to City Hall to get sworn in.

Running was the order of each day. We ran three miles each morning at 8:00 o'clock. We ran two miles every afternoon at 1:00 o'clock. We ran two miles every evening at 4:30. It seem like we were always running. What is the rush?

I remember needing to use the restroom during class. I stood and for no reason and in full sprint, ran out of the class and down the hall to the restroom. My instructor thought that the incident was humorous.

"You must have really needed to go huh, Officer Givens?" he laughed.

During the eighteen weeks of the stressful academy, more than half of the recruits dropped out or were released by the department. Twenty of us graduated and only sixteen made it past field training.

Within four months, I moved my family into a larger and nicer apartment in the hills above Oakland. I had just completed field training and was given my own beat in East Oakland. I was nervous at the beginning of my first day alone in my own police car but the nerves promptly disappeared when I received my first call from dispatch.

The first three years seemed to fly by. Denise and I had been having marital problems rooted mostly in the fact that she wanted me to quit the department and that I had little time to spend with her.

I, on the other hand wanted to continue working because I enjoyed the job. I worked a lot of overtime just to be away from home. This exacerbated the problem because Denise would complain that I was never at home.

I had worked the graveyard shift during this time and my body was just getting used to the hours. The common name for the graveyard shift among law enforcement professionals is "dog watch".

All in all, I thought that I was doing a pretty good job. Many residents on my beat knew and respected me. They felt comfortable approaching me with their problems.

The residents of one home in particular were frequent callers. There were at least eleven people living there in this large Victorian home.

One of them was a nineteen year old young lady whose name was Lydia. Lydia was the mother of a beautiful five month old infant. The baby had huge brown eyes and was the only one in the house that liked me. The father was a guy whose name was Lance.

Lance, who was a convicted felon, could not accept the fact that Lydia had ended their relationship. He would come to the house almost nightly and threaten everyone in the house with death. He would also shoot up the house with his gun. I had never met Lance because he was always gone by the time I reached the house.

One Tuesday at about 2AM, I again received a call of gunshots being fired at Lydia's home. The call originated from a neighbor. It took me about five minutes to arrive at the house and when I did, I was surprised that no one ran out to my patrol car from the house. Usually, I would be met at the curb by Lydia and a company of screaming brothers, cousins and a host of other relatives.

I got out of my car and walked up to the house. I knocked at the door and noticed that it was ajar. I walked into the house and saw one of Lydia's male cousins sleeping on the couch and another on the floor next to the couch in the living room. Both were securely wrapped in blankets in order to keep warm on this cool night.

In the rear of the house, I heard the baby screaming at the top of her little lungs. I decided to let the cousins sleep and I walked to the rear bedroom to check on the baby.

What I saw in that room was horrifying. The five month old infant had been shot in the face. The bullet had gone through one cheek and out the other and she screamed a scream unlike any other scream that I have ever heard in my life. She franticly crawled around a large blood soaked bed.

On the far side of the bed on the floor laid Lydia who had been shot in the head.

I ran back into the living room in order to wake up the cousins. That's when I noticed that both were dead because of gunshot wounds to the head. I walked into another bedroom where there three more dead relatives.

It suddenly occurred to me that maybe I should call for cover or at least unholster my gun just in case the suspect was still on the property.

In all, there were seven dead people in the house. All at the hand of Lance who had even shot his own sweet little five month old daughter in the face.

I called for cover and within minutes there were a dozen or so police units at the house. A neighbor three houses away called and reported that a strange man was in the crawl space underneath her house. I requested a Canine unit to that house and Lance was apprehended and arrested.

That incident was the largest mass murder in the history of Oakland. How could a person have been so cold blooded?

I maintained my professional cool while conducting my preliminary investigation. I was moved to tears when I arrived home that evening. I found it difficult to sleep nights, and when I did sleep I had nightmares about the incident. I could not get the sound of the poor little infant's screams out of my head.

The department agreed to give me ten days off with pay.

I was called to testify in the "Lance" case several weeks after the incident. Just before the trial I met with Deputy DA Wanda Walsh to discuss the merits of the case and my testimony.

Walsh was twenty six years old and gorgeous. She had beautiful long legs that seem to go up to her neck, and big brown eyes.

I found it difficult to concentrate on the case while in her presence. Especially while wearing that medium length black silk dress that exposed those excellently maintained calves.

"Officer Givens... Officer Givens, are you listening to me?"

"Dam, I've been busted looking at those legs." I thought.

"I'm sorry; I was distracted for a minute. What did you say?"

"Officer Givens were you looking at my legs?"

"Guilty as charged. I am throwing myself at the mercy of the court. I am willing to participate in community service or maybe I'll just take you out to dinner for my crime."

She smiled and said, "Your request is denied. I'm going to force you to stand trial first."

"OK... well I would like to exercise my right to a speedy trial."

"You have that right, but I'm the prosecutor, Judge and jury. There will be no defense and there won't be a retrial."

The fact that Denise and I were having problems combined with fact that this beautiful woman and I were actively flirting with each other brought the reality of having an affair to the forefront. I resisted the temptation and did not follow through on my desire to date Wanda.

Things were going so bad at home that Denise and I had separated by the time the three month trial was half over. I subsequently moved into my own apartment in the City of Emeryville, California.

Lance was found guilty of seven counts of murder and one count of attempt murder and was sentenced to death.

Within two months after the trial had concluded, I walked into Wanda's office. She was seated at her desk looking as classy as always.

"Miss Walsh, I was wondering: Is the jury still out on my case?"

"What case are you referring to Officer Givens?" she said as she smiled. She seemed to have known what I was talking about. I was flattered that she remembered my name.

"You know. The felonious leg leer."

She smiled and said, "Yes; you were found guilty as charged and you are sentenced to taking me out tomorrow night. You may pick me up at six. If you're late I'll find you in contempt."

The day of the date, I was as nervous as hell. I had not shared face time with a woman other than Denise in years. I was full of self doubt and I had no idea what we were going to talk about.

I arrived at Wanda's home at 5:55PM. She was gorgeous. She wore a yellow loosely fit short dress. My jaw dropped and I could have sworn that three buttons flew off my shirt when I looked at her.

I wanted to grab her and peel that dress off of her like a banana, but I showed restraint.

We communicated well during the drive to San Francisco's Fairmont Hotel where I had made reservations for dinner. I found that we had much in common and had similar interest and backgrounds. I was pleased to find that my predate nervousness was unfounded.

We made plans to go to Napa Valley's wine country the next day which was on a Sunday. I enjoyed her company and after sampling wine at more than a dozen wineries in Napa Valley, my distorted vision caused me to see two identically dressed Wandas talking to me at the same time. She found it necessary to drive me and my car back home.

"You aren't going to take advantage of me and my body because I've had too much wine, will you." I said jokingly.

"Nope"

"You know, because I am very vulnerable right now"

"Yea, I bet you are."

"It probably wouldn't take much for you to have your way with me right now."

"Oh... you mean that I won't have to knock you in that round bald head first."

"Now that's just kinky. I guess you will first want to handcuff me to the bed too, huh?"

I had never before met anyone like Wanda. Our friendship grew deeper every time we spent time together.

Within months, my divorce was final and Wanda and I had decided to move in together. We agreed to find a two or three bedroom apartment. We needed the extra room because Denise and I had joint custody of Mike Jr. We decided to rent a very nice three bedroom condo in the Oakland hills.

Wanda and I were blissfully happy in our relationship for about one year before I decided to ask her to marry me.One evening, with ring in pocket and while Wanda was taking a bubble bath, I walked into the bathroom carrying two glasses of champagne. Wanda took a bubble bath every evening when she arrived home from work. It was a stress reliever after a long day at the district attorney's office.

"Hi sweetie. How was your day?"

"Hello baby. Is that champagne you have there? It's amazing. You know you are the sweetest man in the world. I don't know what I would do without you in my life. I don't even want to think about it."

I handed her one of the glasses as I sat on the tub's edge. "Do you really mean that, because I'm going to quote you on that later?"

"Why do you ask? Do you have doubts?"

At that point I stood up, reached into my pocket, removed the ring and presented it to her on bended knee.

"Sweetheart, I love you dearly and I want to spend the rest of my life with you. Will you marry me?"

Wanda screamed and cried uncontrollably. She then grabbed my new silk tie that I wore and pulled me into the tub with her. I was wearing my favorite suit. The next thing I knew, she had ripped my soaked clothes off of my body and flung them across the bathroom. She didn't even bother unbuttoning my shirt. Buttons were flying all over the room.That was a good night.

"Yes Mike Givens, I will marry you."

I then heard the doorbell ring. I remembered that I had ordered a pizza before I proposed to Wanda. I jumped out of the tub, put on my robe, grabbed my drenched wallet from my soaked pants and paid for the pizza with a waterlogged twenty dollar bill.

The delivery man didn't seem to mind. I guess a wet tip is just as good as dry one.

Yes, even though I had ruined a perfectly good suit, this was a good day. I think that I maintained a constant smile on my face for a week.

Wanda was the love of my life and I had decided that I would not make the same mistakes I had made in my first marriage. I was much too young and immature when Denise and I married. I was a twenty one year old police officer without enough willpower to resist the constant advances of beautiful women that were attracted to me merely because of the uniform.

That was years ago and I was now mentally much stronger. I loved Wanda with all my heart. My life had never been better. My job was secure and I was happy. What more could a man ask for?

3

WANDA

1 L72" squelched the police radio in my patrol car. 1L72 was the radio call sign of my sergeant.

"1L72 go ahead" responded the dispatcher.

"72, can you have 1L10 meet me at W.MacArthur and Telegraph Ave."

"1L10" inquired the dispatcher.

"1L10" I responded.

"1L10, please meet 1L72 at W.MacArthur and Telegraph"

"1L10 copy"

"I wonder what sarg wants" I thought as I drove to Telegraph Ave. I honestly though he wanted to complement me on my fantastic performance on the job. Boy was I wrong.

"Hello Mike. How's it going?"

"I'm good sarg what's up?"

"Mike, I've been monitoring your radio transmissions and I'm disappointed in the number of people you stop during your shift. Do you have a problem with stopping folks walking down the street?"

"What do you mean sarg? In the academy I was trained that I have the right to stop a person if I have probable cause that a crime has been or is being committed.

"In this neighborhood at two o'clock in the morning, everyone on the street has committed a crime or about to commit a crime."

"I don't believe that sarg. If I weren't wearing this uniform and were walking home from my girlfriend's house, I would not expect to be stopped by the police. Regardless of what neighborhood I was in."

"Well, here in the real world and on this department, we stop everyone."

"Sorry sarg, I won't do it, unless you are planning on changing the U.S. constitution."

That meeting was pivotal in my career as a police officer. Sgt. Henderson was part of the ole boy racist network of cops that at one time made up a majority of the department.

He spread rumors throughout the department that I was not doing my job and that I was soft on criminals. The fact that some other sergeants did not want me in their squads made my job a little more difficult over the next few years. But I managed.

But life at home was great. For the past three weeks, Wanda had been very busy prosecuting a homicide that took a great deal of her time.

Wanda loved the cheese cake served at a local restaurant so I thought I'd surprise her by bringing the delicious dessert home.

When I walked into the apartment, I saw Wanda sitting at the dining room table buried in a pile of law books. I went into the kitchen, sliced a hefty serving of the tasty dessert and presented it to her. She smiled and gently grabbed my ears and kissed my lips.

"Hi sweetie. Thank you. Once again you have read my mind. I was just thinking about eating something sweet. I think that you want me to get fat."

"Yeah... that's what I want. Another two or three hundred pounds on you and I'd be a happy man. Can you help me out?"

"I don't know about two or three hundred pounds, but I think I can meet you part of the way. I think that I may be pregnant." She said nervously.

IF YOU WANT TO MAKE GOD LAUGH, TELL HIM WHAT YOUR PLANS ARE.

Wanda and I had discussed several times the possibility of having a child, but we both decided to wait a year or two, until after we had purchased a home. I was thrilled and excited that God had other plans for our lives.

It took about ten seconds for her words to sink in. I knelt next to the chair that Wanda sat and held her hand. A tear rolled down her face and her eyes lit up like two Christmas lights as I caught her gaze.

"Wanda, you know that I love you very much. You are the love of my life and I would cut off my right arm for you."

"But you are left handed", she said jokingly as more tears fell down her face.

"OK... both arms. Someone once told me that if you want to make God laugh, tell him what your plans are. Well God's plan is that we have this baby and nothing would make me happier."

"Mike, I love you too and I hoped that you would feel this way about my pregnancy. I hope that the baby looks like you."

"Ok, you want a bald headed little girl?"

"Stop... you know what I mean. Besides you won't be able to help me with the baby anyway."

"Why not?"

"Because you'll have no arms."

"Very funny. I'm keeping my arms so that I can hug you when you gain those three hundred pounds. By the way, do you have an appointment with your doctor to have a pregnancy test?"

"Yes I do. I have an appointment tomorrow afternoon. Are you coming with me?"

"I would not miss it for the world."

The day of the appointment, I got off work two hours early so that I could be with Wanda on this important day.

After a two hour wait at the doctor's office, Wanda was called by the nurse to go to the examination room. I wanted to go with her but the tall husky female nurse objected to my persistence. I thought that she wanted to hurt me and she looked as if she could, so I relented. The examination only took a few minutes.

On the drive home, Wanda and I discussed what we would name the baby. I was partial to Marvin if the baby was a boy or Shirley if it was a girl. Shirley is my mother's name. Wanda liked the names Darnell and Eve. We agreed to continue this conversation at a later date.

The next day Wanda called me on my brand new brick cell phone and asked that I meet her for lunch. I arrived at her office at noon. I noticed Wanda sitting at her desk as I walked up the corridor. She hadn't yet noticed me as she sat there with her head buried in a law book. she was smiling from ear to ear. I knew then that she had gotten good news from her doctor.

As I approached the door of her office she turned toward me and immediately rose. She reached up and wrapped her arms around my neck and rested her head on my chest.

"I've been sitting here trying to concentrate on this case, but I can't get you off my mind. You are interfering with my job performance."

"I would feel guilty if the guy you are prosecuting was found to be not guilty, so maybe you should skip lunch and get some work in."

"Not on your life officer. You are not getting out of this so easily. You ARE going to take your gorgeous pregnant fiancé to lunch"

"Have you...."

"Yes, I've heard from the doctor. You are going to be a daddy."

This was one of the happiest days of my life. While eating lunch, we discussed our wedding and made plans for our future together. We had decided to, within a year, have a small ceremony in the Oakland hills at Wedding Point. Thousands of weddings have taken place at Wedding Point as it was perfect for small ceremonies. There is a gazebo near a cliff with the backdrop of the San Francisco Bay Area. It is a photographers dream. The view is phenomenal.

There was no doubt in my mind that Wanda was the love of my life and I was willing to let nothing come between us.

I had begun teaching traffic school to earn extra money so that Wanda and I could buy a home.

I really enjoyed teaching. I felt that I was doing something worthwhile even though absolutely no-one wanted to be in the classes. My injection of humor made the classes tolerable for most of the students.

After teaching for two months, I decided to open my own traffic school. I obtained the required application forms from the State of California, paid the fees, and within four month I was the owner of a licensed traffic school. My next task was to set up an office and hire instructors.

Six months later, I had classes set up in eight area cities and employed eleven instructors. The traffic school was earning more than I was making from the police department.

Wanda and my plans were really coming together nicely and we both were excited about the birth of the baby. Even my son, Mike Jr., who was then six years old, was excited about the prospect of having a little brother or sister.

One day while on patrol, Sgt Henderson requested a meeting with me. I thought that the request was odd because he was no longer my supervisor.

"Howzit goin Mike?"

"It's going sarg, watsup?"

"Mike, I understand that you have opened your own traffic school"

"Yes I did"

"Well you are going to have to close it. You can't write someone a ticket and then make money from them when they go to your school. That's a conflict of interest." He said smugly, and then drove away.

I left that meeting feeling mad as hell. How dare this sergeant approach me this way? Especially considering the fact that he was no longer my supervisor.

Apparently he had heard that my school was doing well and just wanted to antagonize me. Dam playa hater.

But regardless of his motives, I suddenly had a decision to make. I could either close my business or quit the department. At the time, I was making much more money running the business than I earned at the police department. But the idea of being out there on my own without benefits or job security frightened me. Especially considering the fact that we were expecting a baby.

I was determined to put off making this career decision until after the baby was born. Wanda was now nearly at term and though she was nearly as big as a house she was still as beautiful to me as she was the day we met. She had taken leave from the district attorneys' office and because of a difficult pregnancy was instructed by her doctor to remain in bed as much as possible.

"2-Adam11," the feminine voice on the radio sounded one afternoon while I was on routine patrol.

"Adam11," I recanted.

"Adam11, please call the desk sergeant at your earliest convenience "

"Oh boy... here we go", I thought. I was convinced that Sergeant Henderson had told my supervisor about my Traffic School and now my sergeant wanted to talk to me about closing it. I pulled over at the first pay phone I saw and called the sergeant.

"Hello sarg. This is Mike Givens. Radio instructed me to call you."

"Hi Mike. We received a call from St. Regis Hospital. Wanda is in labor. You are excused to go there if you wish."

I immediately dropped the phone, raced to my patrol car, activated my red lights and siren, and drove code 3 to St. Regis Hospital.

My only regret was that I arrived at the hospital too late to see the birth of my nine pound three ounce son that Wanda and I named Byron.

Byron was beautiful and had a cone shaped head that the doctors informed me would round itself in a few days. Wanda, whose gorgeous head was still perfectly round, was also doing well.

Wanda and I brought Byron home from the hospital the very next day. I had taken Mike Jr. to the hospital with me in order to introduce him to his new little brother.

Little Byron was the mirror image of Mike Jr. at birth except for the cone head. Wanda was so excited about being a new mom that I could not keep her from crying.

I used five vacation days from my job so that I could stay at home and take care of Wanda and the baby. For those five days I waited on Wanda hand and foot. It was the least that I could do for her for giving me such a wonderful gift.

Not a day went by that I did not thank God for my little family. There were times that I stood above Byron's crib staring at him while he slept at two or three o'clock in the morning waiting for him to wake up so that I could play with him.

Wanda and I had discussed the possibility of my quitting the police department and running my school full time. I still had reservations which were mostly rooted in fear. Fear that I would not have benefits. Fear that I wouldn't have a steady paycheck. Fear that I wouldn't have the security of a dependable and reliable job. Fear that the business might fail.

"Mike, I have confidence in you and faith in God that the business will continue to be successful and that our family will prosper. So if you feel secure in the fact that you are doing the right thing by quitting the police department, I'm one hundred percent behind you."

I needed to hear Wanda say that. The next day, I gave my lieutenant my two week notice. I was placed on desk duty the duration of my time on the department.

JANUARY 3, 1992

For the first time since I was twenty one years old, I did not have the Oakland police department to fall back on. It was a strange feeling. I could no longer legally carry a firearm. That feeling of assumed power that I once had over the average citizen was suddenly gone. Not to mention the fact That Wanda and I could no longer attend movies free or dine for half price or free at popular restaurants. However, I resigned from the job with my health, piece of mind and self respect and that meant a lot to me.

Within eight months, the size of my traffic school had doubled in size with twelve branches in twelve different cities. Life was good. Businesswise, most of my time was spent training new instructors and other administration duties. My business life was great. My family life fulfilling, and I was happy.

I thought nothing in my life could go wrong.

LIFE IS WHAT YOU MAKE IT.... BUT
SOMETIMES LIFE IS HOW YOU TAKE IT.

"Happy, happy, joy, joy" said five year old little Byron as he read from his favorite book as he sat on the couch sandwiched between Wanda and me. We could not be happier with Byron's development. He was a brilliant child and seemed curious about everything. He attended day care and enjoyed playing with the other kids.

Wanda and I had purchased a spacious home in Clove, CA. This was the house I had dreamed of for most my life. It had a circular driveway, a gourmet kitchen, and four spacious bedrooms. Two of which were full bedroom suites.

It was near good shopping areas, which made it very convenient for Wanda and it was also just down the hill from St. Elizabeth Elementary school, which is one of the areas top schools and where we wanted Byron to attend. We wasted no time in enrolling Byron in the pre-school program at St. Elizabeth.

Byron was a very sociable and sensitive boy who yearned the attention of his parents. So much so that I thought that he might find it difficult to adjust to his new school.

To my surprise, when I drove up to the school on his first day, Byron, armed with his lunch box and sponge-Bob backpack opened the car door and ran into the school. He never even turned around to look back at daddy.

Byron flew through his pre-school year and was promoted to the first grade. Wanda and I were so proud of our baby as he walked across that stage wearing the little cap and gown and receiving his diploma. Wanda cried like a baby. Coincidentally, there was something in my eye that caused it to leak man tears.

"Mr. and Mrs. Givens", exclaimed a shrill voice behind Wanda and me. When we turned we noticed Byron's preschool teacher, Miss Harden.

"Mr. and Mrs. Givens, I wanted to remind you of the conversation we had several weeks ago concerning Byron taking advanced classes when school resumes in January. I feel that Byron is a very gifted child and I think that he would do well in this new program. Would you be available to meet tomorrow after class?"

"I can meet with you, but Mike has a traffic school class he has to teach tomorrow night."

"Good, I'll see you at four o'clock in my classroom."

That evening we took Byron to his favorite pizza restaurant for his graduation present. He had an appetite unlike any six year old I had ever seen. I was lucky to get two slices of pizza.

The next day we woke to a very cold morning. It was unusually cold for Northern California. Temperatures had dropped below freezing as evident by the ice that seem to cover everything outside. I had heard on the news that temperatures were expected to drop another eight degrees before days end. Wanda was already awake and in the kitchen cooking breakfast for Byron and me. After showering, I walked to the kitchen and stood un-noticed in the doorway staring at Wanda who was then already dressed for work.

I was amazed that she looked exactly the same as the day we had met. She had even lost the extra weight she had gained before she delivered Byron.

"Who is that beautiful woman in my kitchen and why is she wearing my wife's clothes"

"Good morning dear. Could you wake and dress Byron this morning, I'm running late"

"Sure, no problem. Don't forget that you have a meeting with his teacher at four o'clock"

"I won't forget. Gotta go. I'll see you tonight. I love you."

Byron was especially energetic and excited about going to school this day because he was instructed to wear his cap and gown in order to take a class photo.

After eating, I loaded him into my SUV and drove him to St.Elizabeth School.

The pre-school classes were located in the rear of the school so parents were forced to drive up a very steep and muddy driveway that was on the schools property.

On this morning, the ice, water and mud on this path made driving more difficult than usual. The wheels on my SUV spun out of control, but I was ultimately able to bring it under my control and traverse the steep incline.

Byron hopped out of the truck running and slipped on the ice and fell on his butt. With a big smile on his face he returned to his feet and ran up the stairs. Once at the top he turned toward me and waved.

"Bye Daddy."

Traversing down the steep driveway was an adventure unto itself. When I attempted to break to slow down, my truck slid about seven feet on the ice and mud. I was however able to stop at the stop sign where the driveway met the street.

I felt obligated to notify the school of this driving hazard. When I called, the school's principal seemed sympathetic and promised me that she would close the driveway until the ice hazard was over. I was satisfied with her response.

I was met at my office by seven of my instructors who were there to participate in a training session that I had scheduled. I had made arrangements to have lunch with Wanda at one o'clock. I took her to my favorite Chinese Restaurant.

Each and every time I saw Wanda, it was like seeing her for the first time. My love for her grew stronger every day. Sometimes it seemed impossible for me to keep my hands off of her. It took all the will power I could muster to prevent myself from reaching across my Mongolian Beef, grab her and slide her past my egg foo young, dip her in soy sauce and eat her like a chicken wing. I was either very hungry or very horny.

I felt like all my past and failed relationships had prepared me for what Wanda and I shared.

On this day in particular, I was feeling especially drawn to Wanda. Before my traffic school class, I had taken the time to purchase a very nice bottle of wine, incense, and a very, very little pink teddy from Victoria's Secret.

My plan was to wrestle and play with Byron so as to deplete him of all energy. That would guarantee that he would go to bed early.

Then I would run a bubble bath and open the wine and light the candles and incense that encircled the tub. I never forgot the fact that bubbles and bubbly alcohol seem to work every time with Wanda.

The class that I taught began at five that evening and ended at eight. Students were required to attend both Monday and Tuesday sessions.

I arrived home at about eight thirty and was surprised to find that Wanda and Byron were not there. I was disappointed because Wanda had told me at lunch that she would make me a special dinner and I was very hungry. The phone rang. I thought it might have been Wanda, but it was Deborah, Wanda's sister.

"Hi Mike... is Wanda there."

"No she isn't Deb. I just got home and I haven't heard from her yet. Have you talked to her today?"

"No. I tried to call her cell but I get nothing but voice mail. Will you tell her to call me when she gets in?"

"I will. See ya soon."

I thought it odd that Wanda did not answer her sister's calls. Wanda always answered her cell phone whenever possible.

I called her cell. The third ring was interrupted and her outgoing message began. I noticed a beep on the house phone which indicated to me that there were incoming messages on the voicemail. I checked the voicemail.

"Mr. Givens. I am Dr. Wong calling from Bay Hospital. Your fiancé' and son have been involved in a traffic accident......"

I didn't wait around to hear the rest of the message. I drove to the hospital in a mad rush observing few red lights or traffic signs or signals along the way.

Still half dressed; I ran into the bustling emergency room and demanded to speak to Dr. Wong. Several nurses, seeing that I was distressed had little success in calming me.

Finally a gentleman who identified himself as Wong approached and escorted me to a waiting area and asked me to sit.

"Mr. Givens, your wife and son were involved in a traffic accident and I'm sorry to inform you that your son was fatally injured. Wanda was critically injured. She is in surgery as we speak."

"Noooooooo" I yelled at the top of my voice. I felt as if my life force was being sucked out of me as uncontrollable tears streamed down my face. I just got up and paced the room as the doctor continued to speak. I heard nothing he said. It was as if my brain could not absorb any more information. I was emotionally paralyzed.

"Where is she?"

"Like I said, she is in surgery. Our best surgeons have been working on her for the past three hours but it doesn't look good. She has sustained massive head injuries and several broken bones and internal injuries.

Apparently she had just picked up your son from school and slid on ice down a steep muddy driveway and was hit by oncoming traffic. Even though she was wearing a seatbelt, the other car hit her driver's door which caused her head to break the side window. Her car then went through an embankment and down a hill. It took forty five minutes to get them up the hill and out of the car. I'll let you know the moment she gets out of surgery. If there is anything that I can do please let me know."

I sat in the waiting room confused and in stunned disbelief. I blamed myself for not being more aggressive with the school about the driveway. I wanted to tell that doctor yes there is something you can do for me. You can give me my family back. Because without them, I have nothing. My faith in God had been shaken to the core.

What have I done to deserve this? All my years on this planet, I had led an exemplary life. I didn't drink much, I didn't do drugs and I treasured my family more than anything in the world. I had done everything to garner the affection of God and now I felt that he had turned his back on me.

I paced back and forth in that waiting room for what seem to be six hours. An unceasing stream of tears soaked the black tee shirt I wore as I waited for news of Wanda's condition. Finally Dr. Wong entered the room.

"Mr. Givens, Wanda is being moved to intensive care. The surgeons have done everything that they could for her but her injuries are substantial. They were able to stop most of the internal bleeding but most of her major organs have shut down. I'm sorry sir, but Wanda probably won't make it through the night."

I fell to my knees and wept like a baby. Inside my chest I felt my heart breaking.

"I need to talk to my fiancé.

"Sure. Right this way Mr. Givens."

We walked down a long corridor until we reached the double doors that lead into the intensive care unit. I entered the room and noticed Wanda's motionless body laying on the second gurney in this semi-private room. It broke my heart to see Wanda tethered to the many machines which maintained her life. I gently brushed her face with my hand.

I stayed through the night and the following morning. That afternoon, I touched her hand and she responded by opening her eyes slightly for the first time since the accident. Her meager attempt to turn her head in my direction was thwarted by the hard plastic brace that encircled her neck.

"What happened? What am I doing here?" she said in a weak and feeble voice as I gently held her hand.

"Shh... Please don't try to talk. After picking up Byron from school, you were involved in a car crash. Try to relax." I told her as tears rolled down my face.

"Where's Byron? Where's my son?" she said in a barely audible voice.

"He is OK. They are taking good care of him."

I lied to her because I did not want her to suffer any more than she had to in what could be her last day of life. Wanda drifted in and out of consciousness for two and a half hours then passed away in my arms.

I left that hospital a profoundly changed person.

4

LIFE GOES ON

It's ten o'clock in the evening and I am so exhausted that I fell asleep at my dining room table atop a mountain of paperwork. It was the end of the year and I had spent the better part of the day preparing reports for the State of California regarding the traffic school.

I managed to, in a daze, find my way to my bed and fell flat on my back. Wanda curled next to me and kissed me atop my bald head. She placed her head on my chest and told me that she loved me.

I then heard my son Byron walk into the room. He stood at the foot of our bed holding his stomach. Wanda told me earlier that she and Byron had stopped at the ice cream shop before coming home. Evidently Byron ingested too much of the tasty frozen dessert.

"Daddy, my stomach hurts."

"Come here son."

He crawled onto the bed and laid between Wanda and me. We three laid, slept and were happy.

Imagine my consternation moments later when I opened my eyes and found myself gently caressing a cold life

less pillow alone in that room, and on this planet.

I had gone through a wide range of emotions since my family was taken from me.

I found it difficult to reconcile my relationship with God and could not understand why he had done this thing to me. After all, we had attended church weekly and we tried to live within what we thought was God's will in our lives.

Neither Wanda nor I drank alcohol in excess, smoked cigarettes, or did drugs. I could not understand why, in this world full of evil and imperfection, why God chose to take such humanly good and perfection.

For the next six months, I did little but work. I could not bring myself to participate in social events, travel, or include myself in any type of social interaction.

One June evening, there was a knock at my door. I looked through the peep hole and saw my old friend John standing there.

Depressed and filled with self pity, I had decided to ignore his knocks and perhaps he would go away, but John, being the super cop that he is, noticed the interrupted light through the peep hole and knocked again.

"Mike, I know that you are in there. Open the door man."

I opened the door even though I didn't want company and felt generally anti- social.

John and I maintained our friendship over the years. He and his wife, Vanessa had divorced two years prior.

"Wasup John. What's going on?"

"Man get up and get dressed. We are getting out of here."

I guess based on my unshaven unkempt appearance, dirty tennis shoes and sweat pants that it was immediately obvious to him that I had not been out of the house in days.

"Out of here? Why? I have everything I need right here. There is food in the refrigerator and lots to see on TV. Why do I need to leave?"

"Mike, I love ya like a step nephew in law and it pains me to see you like this ."

"Like what?"

"This isn't you. It seems as if your joy of life has been robbed from you. Your motivation has been taken away. It seems like you have just given up on living."

"I have. You don't understand what I'm going through. Wanda and I were on the precipice of a wonderful life together. I waited most of my life for someone like her to come along and I feel like I had been robbed.

"I also feel responsible for the accident and the loss of my family. I would have gladly given my life for theirs. I should have warned her about the muddy driveway. I could have prevented the accident."

"I can't pretend to know or understand what you are going through, but as painful as it is, you will eventually move on. And until you do, I'll be there if you need someone to talk to. Now let's go and get something to eat."

I showered and shaved and we were off to Chevy's Restaurant.

John's company and conversation was very therapeutic. It was the shake I needed to wake me from the daze in which I had walked and it helped to put me back on the path of life.

John had introduced me to a very attractive woman whom he had met at the bar but I thought that it was much too early for me to start dating again so I politely refused her advances.

John suggested that I take a trip somewhere. I thought that was a good idea. I hadn't taken a trip since Wanda and I vacationed in Hawaii. And since I hadn't been back home to New Orleans in at least nine years, I decided to make reservations the next day to spend a week in New Orleans.

I also made a call to my college friend, Larry, who still lived in New Orleans. Larry owned a large private security company. He insisted that I not get a hotel room and stay at his home.

On the surface, the City of New Orleans appeared just as I remembered. The weather was hot and humid, the people were friendly, and the food was good.

Larry and I frequented all of our old favorite restaurants and night spots that we used to hang out in back in the day. During the day while Larry worked, I visited my old High School (L.B. Landry HS), my old college (Xavier University) and the old neighborhood.

I was surprised to discover that most of the fellas I went to high school with were either dead, in prison or seriously strung out on drugs.

The City of Oakland had terrible drug and gang problems but it was nothing compared to the drug and gang situation in The Big Easy. It seemed that the majority of black men were either addicts, incarcerated or dealers.

Larry told me that back in the late 80's, the crack cocaine epidemic really hit New Orleans hard and drug gangs fought over turf in perpetuity. He said that crack had people going crazy.

I had read in the local paper that New Orleans led the country per capita in most serious crime categories including murder. The New Orleans drug gangs were ruthless.

Though I still loved the city, I quickly realized that this was not the same city that I grew up in.

The biggest problem that I had to contend with in high school was marijuana and fist fights. The prospect of killing another student was out of the question.

Modern students have to avoid crack, meth and a myriad of other drugs and guns have replaced fist.

I had always wondered what it was about crack that had everyone insane. I could not imagine anything having that much control of me. I couldn't understand why they just couldn't stop smoking that stuff.

Despite the negatives about the city, it's pretty much a rap that New Orleans is the party capital of the United States. The night clubs were open all night and they are all over the place. It's pretty easy to go a several days without sleeping. I am proof of that.

Overall, my stay in the Crescent City was a positive experience. It allowed me to focus my attention outwardly instead of sitting in my home feeling sorry for myself. I realized that in order to survive, I had to move on.

Larry gave me a ride to the airport for my trip back to Oakland. Along the way he mentioned that he was in the process of reorganizing his business. He had just fired his operations manager and was interviewing in order to hire another one. He asked if I wanted the job and tried to seduce me with perks such as a company car, a free apartment, an expense account and an above average salary.

"You are trippin Larry. Don't you realize that I have a successful business in California?"

"Well, just keep my offer in mind. In case you want to move back home. Hey man... you know it's been good seeing you after all these years. I think that I'm gonna plan a trip to California"

"That'll be cool. You can stay at my house and we will hang out. Thanks for your hospitality buddy."

I got out of Larry's car curbside at the New Orleans International Airport feeling able to move on with my life. This, by far was the best time I'd had since I lost my family in the accident. I gained twelve pounds in seven days by stuffing as much New Orleans cuisine in my face as possible.

During the trip home, I prayed that God would allow Wanda's and Byron's souls to rest in peace and I asked for his guidance and grace in all of my associations and in every phase of my life.

Once back in Oakland, I was met at my door by a letter from the State of California agency that regulates traffic violator schools. The letter itemized several changes that would be implemented in the program.

The most significant of the changes was that those that wished to attend traffic school would have to pay the entire traffic ticket before registering for traffic school. Previously, students would have only had to pay a small fee. Many people would attend traffic school just to get out of paying the ticket. The change meant that the student's only motivation to attend traffic school would be to prevent insurance rates from going up. My income was immediately cut in half because of this change. Within six months, I found it difficult to remain in operation and I eventually closed the business.

Once again, I found myself at a crossroads. However, I saw it as an opportunity to grow and expand my horizons. As I evaluated my options, I remembered Larry's offer to run his business in New Orleans. Another option would be return to the Oakland Police Department. I also had an option of studying Real Estate and becoming an agent.

THE ADDICT IN ME

I am convinced that there is a part of all human brains that responds to the environment and things that happens in our environment the way an addicts brain would. It occurs at differing levels and for different reasons in each individual.

Most people are addicted to something. These addictions manifest themselves as compulsions for things such as shopping, alcohol, food, love, cigarettes, credit, sex, religion, chocolate, men, chocolate men, woman and a multitude of other things.

In fact, I think it fair to say that every person on the planet has compulsions for something. However if our compulsions fall short of becoming obsessions, we are spared the life changing affects of addiction.

We that suffer from the disease of addiction allow these compulsions and obsessions to run and ruin our lives.

ALL ADDICTS HAVE WEAKNESSES BUT NOT ALL WITH WEAKENSSES ARE ADDICTS

I had discovered maybe too late in life, that my weakness is the need for immediate gratification. I did not understand that the ability to build a prosperous life is reliant on the capacity to plan many years in advance. No. I wanted immediate results for any of my actions. I didn't care what would happen in ten years because of any decision I made today.

I am the result of every decision that I ever have made in my life. This fact did not occur to me several years prior when instead of being patient and waiting until after I graduated, I left college to come to California and marry Denise. Nor did this fact occur to me when instead of re-enrolling in school, I decided to join the police department. In both cases, I opted for the result that would bring immediate gratification.

As I look back, I now realize that I had been living my life for the short term, devoid of any long term planning. The addict in me craves "the now."

I was an addict long before I did my first drug.

Someone once said, "If life gives you lemons, make lemonade." Now imagine life giving you lemonade and you proceed to try to make lemons.

That's addict behavior. The addict that lives in me will try over and over again to make lemons from lemonade with negative results. But that doesn't keep him from continuing to try.

Now, the addict that dwells within me <u>knows</u> that each attempt to create a lemon from lemonade will end in futility, but this fact does not deter my addict from trying anyway. It's inexplicable. In fact, the more he fails the more determined he is that he must succeed in making these lemons.

Realizing this fact, I can now quantify the addict in me. And I also realize that the motivation of my inner addict will have very little to do with drugs.

Drugs will be only symptoms of a larger problem. There will be times in my addiction that I will stop using cocaine but my addict (immediate gratification) will still live within me.

It's like treating someone's flu symptoms. You may temporarily impede their coughing, fever, or sniffles by giving him flu medication, but the person still has the flu. By the same token, I may stop using drugs but I will still be an addict.

Unfortunately I will have to put many more years and experiences, many of them life threatening, behind me before I will realize that my addict does not control me. God is in charge.

Another thing I have to realize is that though I had never used drugs at this point in my life, the addict was alive and well in my brain just waiting to catch me slipping.

EASY DOES IT

Alcoholic Anonymous

5

NAW'LINS

D ecisions. Decisions. Should I attend Real Estate school? Should I move back to New Orleans? Should I go back to being a cop? The rational "me" would study Real Estate and build my business for long term wealth. However, my addict had decided to move to New Orleans to run Larry's security company. My addict saw that as the quickest and easiest way to instant gratification. This turned out to be the second biggest mistake of my life.

When I called Larry to ask if the position was still open, he was excited to hear from me and said that his offer still stood. In fact, he told me that he recently obtained a contract for all the Walgreens stores in the Greater New Orleans area and needed me to train his guards, hire new ones, rewrite his training manuals and manage the contract.

I secured the closing of the school and rented out my home. I then filled a U-Haul trailer with the stuff that I decided to take with me to New Orleans, then hooked the trailer to my truck and hit the road Louisiana bound.

Larry had been true to his word. The spacious two bedroom condo he rented for me was beautiful and I had access to an under cover looking car complete with a yellow light bar on top and movable spotlights on either door.

The first months on the job were well spent. I rewrote all the company's training manuals and scheduled each guard in my region for training classes which I taught.

NIKKI

My social life began to pick up also. I dated casually, but always managed to stay at least arms length of relationships.

There was one young lady in particular that captured my eye. She lived with her mother in the same complex that I lived. I had spoken to her occasionally and casually in the parking lot of the apartment complex but had never met her formally. The only thing that I can remember about her is that she had great legs.

I answered a knock at my door and through my peep hole saw her standing there. I opened the door and immediately noticed the sneaky smile on her face.

"I decided to take action. I have seen you in the parking lot several times and casually spoken to you a couple of times." She said with a heavy New Orleans accent.

"Well, I'm glad you did. I've wanted to meet you."

"Well I can't tell. You hardly said anything. By the way, my name is Nikki".

There were two things that immediately bothered me about Nikki. The first was that she was very aggressive. I have never been attracted to an overly aggressive woman. The second thing was the fact that she smoked cigarettes. Though she did not light up in my apartment, I smelled it on her breath.

Despite these two drawbacks, I was willing to spend time with her. I guess she caught me in a transitional period. I was new to the area and knew almost no one. Also, those legs were hard to resist.

"Nikki, I'm making dinner. Are you hungry?"

"I will eat as long as you don't put anything in the food that will knock me out, so that you can take advantage of me"

"My plan exactly. How did you figure me out so fast?"

I made us a delicious meal and we talked as we drank a bottle of wine. I could tell by our conversation that Nikki and I were destined to be no more than just friends. She was a little bit too much on the wild side for me. I got the impression that she had other men and could never be faithful to one. Yet, I found her company stimulating because she was so friendly and open which is a nice quality I find common in southern women.

We talked and laughed into the wee hours of the morning.

"Mike you are a funny guy"

"Are you surprised that I have a sense of humor"

"Yes. Every time I see you, you are all suited up like a business man and looking all serious. I thought you were just like the next square negro. And every time we spoke you talked so proper."

"Would you like it better if I spoke improper?"

"No, you know what I mean." She laughed.

I realized the late hour and I was about to ask her to leave when she stood and walked toward me. Nikki sat next to me on the sofa again bearing that sneaky smile on her face. She continued glaring into my eyes as if she expected something out of me.

She then reached into her purse and removed a glass tube that was about four inches long that I identified from years of police work as a crack pipe.

"Do you indulge?"She asked.

"Oh, Hell no. Baby you gotta go. I don't allow drugs in my home. I've never used drugs and I never will" I yelled.

"Oh, I sorry. I did not mean to offend you. I thought that you might want to try it with me just once. You won't get hooked if you try it once. Look at me. I smoke it once or twice a week and walk away and work the rest of the week. I apologize again. I will be going now."

My rational mind responded silently by saying, get the hell out of here you hopeless dope fiend. Since Nikki could not read minds what she heard was the addict in me say:

"Wait a minute Satan. Oh excuse me; Nikki. Sit down. Let's talk. How does that stuff make you feel?"

"It has different affects on different people. It makes me horny. I can't get enough sex when I get high.

That was the wrong thing for me to hear. I hadn't had sex since Wanda died.

"Really?" She really caught me off guard with that one. "OK, I'll try it once. You go first."

Nikki prepared a hit for her to smoke. After hitting it, Nikki's pupils immediately dilated and she stood without hesitating and took all of her clothes off. She then grabbed my hand and led me into my bedroom.

Once there, Nikki prepared a hit for me and told me to inhale. This was the single biggest mistake of my life. A thick cloud of white smoke filled the room and my ears began to ring.

Nikki then asked me to take off my clothes off. When I did, Nikki did things to me that I had only seen done in porno movies. She was like a savage.

After that first hit, my rational mind knew that I was in trouble. The addict in me was in heaven. My addict had found the perfect device for instant gratification. He wanted that feeling again. And again. And again.

Though I had to be at work at seven o'clock, Nikki and I smoked crack till five o'clock in the morning. So much for just once.

That's when I realized that I was in no condition to work, so I called in sick. We continued smoking and at about 9 AM Nikki ran out of crack and had no money.

That was only a minor inconvenience. Armed with my ATM card, I proceeded to my bank and then to the crack man in order to feed my new addict.

My rational mind saw where this was going but was powerless to do anything about it. I was hooked after my first hit.

At about 3 PM, I became disgusted with myself. I had gone through about two hundred of my own dollars and I told Nikki that I refuse to spend any more. I asked her to leave. She reluctantly did so.

After she had gone, it took all of the strength within me to stop myself from leaving my apartment in order to buy more crack. I felt nervous and paced uncontrollably. Finally, after showering, I fell asleep.

It was hectic at work the next day. I had twice as much work to accomplish because I had missed the day before.

I tried to put the previous day into prospective. It was hard for me to believe that I spent nearly a whole day smoking crack like a common dope fiend. Especially since I had been such a choir boy most of my whole life.

My rational mind was determined to place the experience in the past and make it a one time occurrence. The addict in me however, had other plans.

CRACK IS THE DEVIL'S DRUG. ITS ONLY DESIRE IS TO STEAL YOUR SOUL. IT DOES NOT CARE WHO YOU ARE, WHAT OR WHO YOU KNOW, HOW MUCH MONEY YOU HAVE OR DON'T HAVE, OR WHAT YOU THINK. IT JUST WANTS YOU, EVERYTHING YOU ARE AND EVERYTHING YOU HAVE.

Not feeling like cooking, I picked up a po-boy sandwich at Max's, my favorite restaurant. Max was famous for overstuffing his po-boys.

I ordered an oyster po-boy and took it home. There were way too many oysters on this eighteen inch monster dressed with hot peppers, lettuce, tomatoes and onions, mayonnaise and mustard.

I sat at my dining table ready to devour this rascal, but I felt the need to get rid of the smell of crack that still lingered. Lysol disinfectant did the trick. I then sat and ate until I could eat no more. I then put a couple of logs on the fireplace and lit them in order to take some of the nip out of the air. After showering, I sat in my living room to watch television when I heard a knock at the door. I opened it and there stood Nikki, looking guilty.

"Mike, I feel terrible about yesterday. I didn't mean to let our smoking to get out of control. Do you forgive me?"

"Nikki it was not your fault. I made a decision to do what I did. I'm a grown ass man."

"Can I come in?"

My rational self silently replied, "Absolutely not. Have you lost you mind? Do you think that I want a repeat of what happened yesterday?

But the addict in me enthusiastically responded, "Sure come in."

"I would have hated your being mad at me if you were."

No sooner had she sat down did Nikki pulled a small amount of crack. Before I could say anything she broke it in half, placed her half on her pipe and hit it.

I sat there speechless as Nikki placed my half on her pipe, then placed the pipe in my mouth and lit it. Before I knew it, I was again headed to the ATM.

With each hit of the pipe I felt that I was loosing a small part of myself. I felt less in control of my self will. The addict in me was growing stronger and my ability to say no to the drug and to Nikki was becoming weaker.

Each day for the next few days, Nikki came over after I had gotten home from work with a small amount of crack. It did not take long for me to figure out that she just wanted me to get started so that I would buy more. I was powerless to do anything about it.

Within a month, Nikki and I had smoked all the money that I had saved and I was totally dependent on my job for survival. After paying my bills, we smoked up the rest of my salary.

It quickly reached the point that I no longer had the patience to wait two weeks for a check. I needed immediate gratification. I needed to be paid daily, so I bought a professional grade carpet cleaner, loaded it in my truck and drove around the neighborhood cleaning carpets. Business was great. I made two or three hundred dollars per day so I abruptly quit my job and cleaned carpets full time. The addict in me now had full control of my life.

The fact that I made money each day meant that Nikki and I had money to spend on crack everyday. The problem was that without the patience to save some of the money for things like rent, I faced being evicted after two months. For the first time in my life I had no place to call home.

The addict in me did not care. Even if it meant sleeping in my truck, my addict was content. As long as there were drugs available the addict in me complained not.

It took four months for me to realize that with this crack thing, my life was going nowhere but down the drain. During this period, I lived, ate and worked out of my truck. It was then when I realized that I had to leave New Orleans.

I had lived in California nearly eleven years and never once used anything stronger than aspirin. Then I moved to Louisiana and within two months I'm smoking crack heavily.

I had determined that there was absolutely no benefit to getting high and if I moved back to California this tragic drug experiment gone wrong would be over and I could start a whole new life, or at least continued with my old life.

I loaded my carpet cleaning equipment into my truck and began my trek back to Oakland. It was during this period that I learned how insidious my inner addict is.

I figured that if I returned to California, life would be as it was before.

In twelve step programs, this is called a geographical. Moving from place to place hoping that somehow the desire for drugs would diminish or disappear. This plan would have worked too because I was leaving behind my connections, Nikki and old associations.

But the thing that I brought back to California with me was the addict in me. I should have left his ass in the French Quarter.

The addict in me was gaining strength. In fact the addict didn't even wait until I arrived in California. My addict instructed me to purchase crack in every large city along the I-10 corridor between New Orleans and Oakland. I was powerless to refuse even though I had no desire to smoke crack. I don't really remember the trip. I was high the entire time.

On my extended drive to Oakland, I recalled a time in New Orleans when I sat in a crack house. I remember feeling uncomfortable because the guy sitting directly across from me at the table in this crowded house was staring at me. I had learned from my relatively brief period on the streets of New Orleans that stares should be challenged because if they are not the person doing the staring or others will take advantage of you in any way possible.

"Hey man, you got a problem wit me or are you looking at me like that because you are gay?" I said in a very serious voice.

"No my brother and excuse me for staring. I'm just concerned for you well being. If you don't mind my asking, how long have you been smoking this shit?"

"A cupla months. Why do you want to know ?"

"I see. I hope you don't mind my telling you that you have made the biggest mistake of your life. You might not realize it now because you are in what's called the honeymoon period of your addiction. Right now you are enjoying the high you get when you take a hit and you probably are thinking that you are choosing to get loaded, but you are not. The honeymoon will last up to a year. Then it goes from being a pleasure to being a burden. A burden that you carry around with you 24-7. The fun is over and you're hooked. The silly part about the whole ordeal will be that your brain will think that you're still having fun. That's the insanity. My advice to you would be to do anything but smoke this shit. Drink heavily or pop pills. Anything but this shit. It's too late for me. You see, I've been smoking this shit for twenty four years.

I've lost the woman I love, my family, two houses, cars and every thing and everyone that I hold dear because I chose to smoke this shit. I've even lost myself several times. It's not too late for you."

His advice went in one ear and out the other. After all; I was on my honeymoon.

6

THE ROAD TO HELL

Samuel Johnson once said, "The road to hell is paved with good intentions." With my drug life behind me, my plans were to raise money by cleaning carpets in California. Then I would be able to obtain a license to operate my own security company.

I also had plans to rebuild my relationships with my family, especially my son whom I had not seen in about a year. I was determined to not let anything stop me. I had started reading self-help books and subscribed to security industry periodicals.

I went out of my way to meet other security executives and I attended seminars and conventions.

If you want to make God laugh, tell him what your plans are.

Yet it seemed that God wasn't the only one laughing. The addict in me was having a belly roller at my expense.

Two months had gone by and I entertained no thoughts of getting high. I had to move into my mother's home in Pinole, Ca. because the bank foreclosed on my Oakland house when I made no payments from New Orleans.

Armed with a carpet cleaning machine, I took my craft to the streets of Oakland.

My sales pitch was simple. I would drive around in my truck until I noticed a homeowner on or near his property. I would then get out of my truck and make an offer to him to allow me to clean his carpet at a very attractive price.

This technique had never failed me. I also had magnetic car door signs made with, "Carpet Man" and my cell number printed on them.

YOU WANT TO MAKE GOD LAUGH? TELL HIM WHAT YOU PLANS ARE.

Well, God must still be rolling around heaven in laughter over the blueprint of my life that I laid out before him. I was well on track of being able to open my security company within six months. However the addict that thrived within me had other plans. This cunning, baffling and powerful force was always laying in wait, ready to blindside me at the first opportunity that presented itself.

This day started innocently enough. At seven o'clock, I got out of bed, turned the heater on, and got back in the bed until the room was warm enough. By seven thirty, I'm in the kitchen pouring myself a cup of coffee and eating pancakes, eggs and beef sausage. I went to the garage and loaded my equipment into my truck, kissed my mom on the cheek and away I went.

I decided to work a North Oakland working class neighborhood. Experience had shown me that rich neighborhoods were no good because those residents were not concerned about getting a good deal and usually had a service to clean their carpets.

In very poor neighborhoods the homes are filled with renters whose occupants had little discretionary dollars.

The money is with the working class.

I stopped at a little coffee shop on Martin Luther King Blvd. to get a cup of java. I was met at the front door by a gentleman who had read the sign alongside my truck.

He explained that he owned several pieces of property in the area and one of them was in desperate need of carpet cleaning. He asked me to follow him to the property. I did so.

The female renter was surprised to see the landlord at the door. When she opened the door, a wall of crack smoke gushed from the opening and three or four very excited looking individuals emerged, tweaked their way out of the apartment and gurped their way down the street.

The owner went into the apartment and started yelling at the tenant, threatening to evict her. He then went through the unit and opened all the windows to expel the crack smell before inviting me in. The carpet was filthy and worn beyond cleaning. I told the owner that the carpet needed replacing. He told me that he couldn't afford to have it replaced and told me to do the best I could.

We agreed upon a price and I started the job.

While I worked, the female tenant found it necessary to lock herself in the bathroom. I heard the repeated sound of a striking cigarette lighter coming from the bathroom.

While I worked, I thanked God that I did not have to put myself through the misery that crack would bring. No longer would I wake up broke after having a pocket full of money the night before. No longer would I have to be concerned that someone would knock me in the head and take my possessions.

When I was done with the carpet, I knocked on the bathroom door to inform the tenant that I was through. She opened the bathroom door. It was so smoky in there I could barely distinguish her silhouette. I asked her not to walk on the carpet until it was dry.

"Do you want a hit?" she said.

I am not sure about the existence of the being that some people refer to as the devil. Nor am I sure of the existence of supernatural forces that try to negatively influence our thinking and actions when things are going well in our lives.

Maybe it's a coincidence that every time things start going well in my life, out of the blue someone will make an offer such as the one made by this female that I did not even know.

How did she even know that I had ever smoked crack? During the time that I was in active use of cocaine, no one had ever offered me free crack with the exception of Nikki. But every time I sobered up, people would give it away like it was candy. This can't be a coincidence.

"Yes." I said without hesitation.

WHEN THE ADDICT IN ME ATTACKS, THERE ARE USUALLY WARNING SIGNS. I RECOGNIZE THEM YET JUST HADN'T LEARNED TO.

I ended up getting loaded with her for about three hours; I was totally disgusted with myself. Even though I had not spent any of my own money, I felt like the previous two and a half months were a lie.

I drove to the Berkeley Marina, parked my car and walked along the water's edge yelling loudly at myself. I cared not that people were looking and listening to me. I felt that I could no longer trust my decision making. I needed help, but I didn't know where to go. I sat on a large rock and cried and drowned in a pool of my own self pitty.

I prayed and asked God to help me find a way out of this hole that I had dug for myself.

After leaving the Marina, I stopped at a supermarket to buy something for dinner. I overheard two women in the check out line in front of me talking about a twelve step program. The next day, I called the hotline and found a meeting close to my home. God had answered my prayer.

The meeting was held in the conference room at a church. There were about twenty-five people there who were suspiciously happy considering the fact that they were addicts.

They spoke of their experiences, strengths and hope for the future. Some of these people had been sober for thirty or thirty five years.

I both envied them for being able to maintain sobriety such a long period of time and wondered why they weren't cured after being in that program so long.

These were the first sober addicts I had ever met. I did not know that they existed. I had begun to think that I had a life sentence with no possibility of parole.

MICHAEL C. GIVENS

After the meeting, I spoke to one member and I told him of some of my experiences. He told me that my story is similar to the stories of other addicts who have recovered.

"Recovery is not an event. It is a process. The process begins when you become honest with yourself, maintain an open mind and remain willing to work for your sobriety." He said

He also told me that the process ends the day you die.

"If you do these things and work the 12 steps you will find what you seek. If you need a residential program, I would recommend the Salvation Army. I went through their program years ago. That's where I first got sober and started working the steps."He said.

I didn't think that I needed a residential program but I visited Salvation Army the next day and spoke to the intake manager whose name was Cliff.

Cliff was a huge man. He was as tall as I am but he weighed at least 400 pounds.

He briefly told me his story and his battles with alcohol.

"I commend you for attempting to arrest your addiction in the early stage."He said. "I've been drinking since I was twelve years old. Both my father and mother were alcoholics and my father's father was an alcoholic. It's been my experience that addicts have to hit bottom before they ever can hope to turn their lives around. It's unfortunate that many times we have to loose everything before we admit that we are powerless over the mind and mood altering substances that we put

93

into our bodies. Here at Salivation Army, we offer a safe environment to live in while you recover. This is a working program. You will be expected to work eight hours a day either on one of our trucks, in one of our stores, or on the dock. Is this something that you think you'd be interested in?"

"I am very impressed with the facility, but right now I don't think a residential program is right for me."

"Why not? Do you think you have your addict under control?"

"Yeah... well right now I do."

"Do you? How long do you think that control will last? The problem is that you think that you choose to get high. Nothing is further from the truth. The decision has already been made even if you don't realize it. Your brain is just waiting for the best time to implement the decision."

As he spoke my mind drifted to the young lady in the crack laden apartment whose carpet I cleaned. I wasn't thinking of getting high. The instant she asked me if I wanted a hit, the word yes came out of my mouth even though I had no desire to get high. If she hadn't offered, I wouldn't have used. But eventually someone would offer again or I would be in a situation that would tempt me beyond my control.

"OK... but how can Sally (Salvation Army) help me?"

"We offer support groups, classes in addiction studies, and counseling. But above all, we offer you time. Time that you can perfect your personal plan for your sobriety."

"I need time to think about all of this. I have your card. I'll call you when I make up my mind."

I walked out of Cliff's office not knowing what to do. I knew from experience that regardless of my confidence level now, I would probably use again and soon. I sat parked outside of Sally's offices for an hour before walking back into Cliff's office.

"Cliff. Sign me up!"

SALLY

Overall, Sally was a positive experience. Early on in the program I was asked to be the lead desk officer; which meant that I would have a supervisory position over my fellow addicts in the program.

My first reaction was to say no. The purpose for my coming to Sally was to get better. I did not want to be responsible for any one but myself or any ones problems but my own.

I eventually said yes because the work at the front desk was much easier than working on the dock and the job also came with a private room. Before I accepted the job I had been sleeping in a four man dorm room.

The routine at Sally was rigorous. Everyone in the program had to work at least 40 hours at his assign job, then attend the process groups and classes and also attend one twelve step meeting per day. The program was six months long.

I somehow managed to find time to place my situation into perspective. My counselor had suggested that I was still in denial about my loosing Wanda and Byron. He suggested that I had not mourned properly, and that contributed to my acting out with self destructive behavior. He said that I had become my own worst enemy.

He also pointed out that the years before the accident were filled with successes in our lives and each year we would build on those successes. Since the accident, there was one failure after another. I had lost everything.

After my six month stint at Sally, I was anxious to move on with my life and to start building a future. Within two months I was working sixteen hours a day managing two full time jobs.

One of them was at a high rise hotel in downtown Oakland where I was the assistant security director. The other was as a mobile security guard at a business park in Emeryville Ca.

In a relatively short period of time, I had rented a small apartment and had begun saving money again. I still maintained my regiment of attending one twelve step meeting per day. Things were really beginning to look up.

7

REMY

Such was the case one day while at work at the hotel. The front desk radioed that a guest had locked her room key in her room. Armed with a master key, I responded to the guest's room.

As I approached I noticed a young woman standing

near the locked door. She looked at me with those huge brown eyes and smiled. I was stuck.

"I sure am glad to see you. I was on my way to a seminar when I noticed that I had left my room key in my room. Thank you for coming so quickly."

"Believe me, it's my pleasure. What seminar are you attending?"

"I am a member of the BLSANA. That's the Black Law Students Association of North America. Our national convention is here in Oakland this year."

"Really, where are you from?" I asked as I opened her room door.

"I'm from Seattle Washington."

"Do you know anything about Oakland?" I asked as I looked into those lovely eyes.

"No, this is my first time here. As a matter of fact, I'm going to be here for five days and I was hoping to find a good tour guide."

"You have just found one. And you won't even have to tip me. Much. What kind of food do you like?"

"I think that I want to try some Oakland cuisine." She said with a smile.

"I don't think there is such a thing as Oakland food. Would you settle for some southern Creole Cajun cooking? I know this restaurant that makes the best gumbo this side of the Mississippi."

"Well, if I can't have Oakland food, I guess that'll work. Is six o'clock good for you?"

"Six is perfect. I'll come to your room. Oh... by the way, what's you name?"

"My name is Remy. What's yours?"

"I'm Mike. Meeting you has been a pleasure Remy. I'll see you tonight at six."

At 5:59PM, I knocked at Remy's door. She opened it and there stood this vision of beauty, the likes of which have rarely been seen by any one in my lifetime, or any other lifetime, on this planet or any other planet in this

Universe or any other universe in this or any other parallel dimension. She looked good .

She wore a very classy short black dress and very little makeup. I've never been attracted a woman that wears a lot of makeup.

Even though she possessed a great deal of physical beauty, it was difficult for me to get past those big brown eyes. When she looked at me it was if she looked right through me and they reacted to my every expression.

I heard it said that eyes are windows to our souls. I spent our entire dinner trying to open those windows so that I could touch her soul. Yes... I was smitten.

It was not all physical. We connected on a seemingly spiritual level. She told me so. I was very please to discover that Remy felt about me the same way I felt about her.

After dinner, I took her to a dance club. The problem with clubs is that it's' difficult to hear and I really wanted to talk and get to know Remy, so after about ten minutes we left the club and drove to the marina and parked along side the water.

I had forgotten what it was like to have an adult sincere conversation with a woman. The kind of conversation that Wanda and I once shared. Communicating with Remy reminded me of how Wanda and I once communicated. She and Wanda had similar interest .

"Mike... Mike, are you OK?" She asked as she curiously poked my shoulder.

"Oh, yeah I'm alright. I was just distracted for a second."

"Yes you were. We were talking, and suddenly you seemed to be in a trance as you stared out of the window."

"Please forgive me. It was nothing. I just drifted off to thoughts of my family."

"Oh... I didn't know you had a family."

"Well I did have a family. My wife and son were killed in a car crash a couple years ago."

"I'm sorry."

"It's OK. I still think about them often. They were my reason to live. It was rough for a while, but things are getting better now. But still I miss them a lot. I wake up sometimes at night thinking that the accident was some kind of nightmare. At night I sometimes feel her next to me in bed. I guess I'm not totally over it yet."

"Mike, you may never get over that. Your family was a part of you. No one that close to me has ever past away so I don't propose to know how you feel, but I have a twelve year old daughter that I am raising and if I were to lose her I would imagine it would be like having an arm or leg chopped off."

"Yeah, it's sorta like that but much more painful. I hope you don't mind me saying this, but you remind me of Wanda. You both have a lot in common. You are in law school and she was a deputy district attorney for the county."

"Oh, she was a lawyer?"

"Yes, that's how we met. She was the DA and I was a cop. We worked on a case together. The rest is history."

"I can tell that you really cared about her"

"I loved her very much. Ever since the accident, I've found it difficult to start new relationships. In fact, I think that this is the first real date I've been on since the accident."

"Well, if you ever need a friend to talk to, you can always call me in Seattle."

"Thank you. That means a lot to me. I think that I'll keep you"

"As a friend of course."

"Yeah, that too. I think that I better get you back to your room. You have an early day tomorrow don't you."

"You are not getting rid of me that easily. Where can we get some good ice cream?"

"It's not easy being your tour guide. Maybe you should tip me."

Remy laughed. I took her to a late night creamery that specialized in huge banana splits. I recommended that she should get a regular size split, but she ordered the big one.

In my whole life, I had never seen such a little lady eat so much ice cream.

"Why are you looking at me like that? I told you that ice cream is my weakness." She said laughingly.

"Weakness? I thought that you were going to lick the plate. I was afraid to reach across the table. You would have bitten off my hand. You ate that banana split like a savage."

Remy and I sat there talking until after closing time. We finally left at the request of the manager. I drove Remy to the hotel and walked her to her room.

Once at the door, I wished her a good night and gave her a hug. I didn't want to ruin the entire evening by being too aggressive, but when I looked into those lovely brown eyes, I just had kiss her. And I did.

Finally and reluctantly, I tore myself from her embrace. I made arrangements to see her the next day and I headed home.

The next day was Saturday. Remy had a seminar that ended at noon. I was off work from my second job at two thirty. I picked Remy up and told her that I had a surprise for her at my apartment.

Once there, I went to my refrigerator and removed a strawberry Ice cream cake with an inscription on top that read "To My New Friend, Remy" and I presented it to her.

Remy was speechless. Her eyes lit up like candles. I was thrilled to see her respond that way.

"I got this for you to show you that I appreciate your friendship and that I am grateful that you listened to me last night."

"Mike, you are so sweet. I only have two things to say. Thank you." She said as she stood on her toes to plant a kiss on my lips. "And where are the saucers and spoons?"

Remy cut a large slice of the cake and tore into it like a wild beast. I had never seen such a personality transformation in a person in my life. When there is ice cream in the vicinity hide you kids and pets.

Remy wiped the ice cream from her fingers, forehead, hair and ears and we left my apartment and went to a Jazz festival that was being held in Berkeley. We had a great time.

Some of my favorite jazz performers were there. I was pleased to find out that Remy enjoyed Jazz as much as I did.

I had to work that night so I had to cut this date short.

I saw Remy everyday until the day I drove her to the airport for her return trip to Seattle.

I called Seattle every available opportunity. Our friendship continued to grow despite the distance between us.

Before long, I began spending one weekend per month in Seattle in order to spend time with Remy and her daughter. Remy would occasionally fly to California to see me but that was difficult because of her school schedule.

My friend, John was getting remarried so I invited Remy to the wedding. The day before the wedding, I picked her up from the Airport and was met at the gate by her warm embrace. I was excited to see her. Remy seemed excited also, but I could tell that she had something on her mind. She seemed distracted.

"Are you OK sweetie?"

"Yes I'm OK. It's been a rough week at school. I am averaging three hours sleep per night."

"Oh that must be it. I thought that you had something on your mind, you know....about us."

"You are very perceptive. There is something I'd like to discuss with you later."

"Well let me know when you are ready to talk. John's bachelor's party is tonight so you can catch up on your sleep tonight while I'm gone."

"Do you think that I'll be able to sleep while you're out getting lap dances from butt naked, bare foot strippers at that party?"

"Come on baby. You know that you are the only one that thrill me. And besides modern strippers wear heals."

"Oh yeah... heals...that makes me feel so much better." She said laughingly. "I don't know how much sleep I'm going to get anyway. I have a test on Monday. I brought books with me."

"Well you better sleep while I'm gone because when I get back, I'm gonna want some of that good ole lovin. Can you dig it?"

"Dig it? What are we back in the 60's? And if you plan to do anything with my body tonight, you better lead with ice cream."

"See... now you're getting all freaky deeky on me. Should I bring whipped cream also?"

"Mike... you are a pervert."

"No, it's not that I'm a pervert. It's that I miss you. I haven't seen you in a couple of weeks. And like Marvin said. When I get this feelin, I need sexual healin."

John's Bachelor's party was off the hook. His best man had rented a huge suite in one of San Francisco's fanciest hotels. There were 40 or 50 guys there. Most of them were Oakland cops. There were also three buck wild, booty butt naked, heel wearing, lap dancing strippers and gallons of alcohol.

Police officers are known for throwing wild parties. Especially when there is alcohol and guns involved. This party was no exception.

I once heard someone speak of being lonely in a crowded room. I hadn't fully understood that expression until this night.

Though the party was crowded and everyone was having a good time, I couldn't take my mind off of my beautiful girl at home.

Needless to say that my stay at this party truncated. I congratulated John and I left the party.

The forty minute drive seemed to take twice as long. I stopped at the ice cream shop and bought my baby her favorite flavor. Banana cream. As I drove home I imagined myself opening the door to my apartment and seeing my apartment illuminated with scented candles.

In this freeway driving dream of mine, I walk into my bedroom and Remy is laying there in my bed wearing that little red teddy that I like so much. The reflections of the candles in her huge brown eyes heighten my excitement. I walk over to her and gently kiss her soft lips. Then... whoops. I'm home. End of dream.

When I opened the door to my apartment, the first thing I saw was Remy. She wore a scarf covering huge rollers and a muumuu. She also had on some kind of thick creamy substance on her face that resembled a Mardi Gras mask and a pair of giant rabbit slippers covered her feet.

She was sitting at my dining room table buried in a pile of books and pecking away at her laptop.

I smiled as I handed her the ice cream. I remember thinking that somehow she has managed to make this outfit look sexy. There was no other place I would rather be.

"Why are you smiling?"she said.

"I'm smiling because you are so beautiful to me."

"You're sick. I look hideous right now. Now I know that you're a pervert."

Again I sensed that Remy had something on her mind that she wasn't telling me. Reading Remy's emotions was very easy to me. Every one of her thoughts and feelings were always expressed in her face and in those eyes.

"Are you ready to talk to me yet?"

Again, she seemed nervous and apprehensive. Her look was pensive as she looked into my eyes.

"Mike...Um... I just wanted you to know that I have fallen in love with you and I wanted to ask you if that was OK."

"Is that it? Are you kidding me? Sometimes that's all I do is think about you. You are the first thing that I think about in the morning and the last thing that I think about before I go to sleep. You have broken down emotional walls that have taken me years to build. I get excited each and every time I think about you. Tonight I was at a party with friends that I haven't seen in years and butt naked dancers wearing heels and all I could do is think about you. I left early and couldn't wait to get here. You are very important to me and I love you very much. I never thought that I could feel this way about someone again. So, is it OK? Yes it is OK. As a matter of fact, I downright recommend it. Did I answer your question?" I looked at her and noticed that her eyes were welled up and tears streamed down her beautiful face. She stood on her toes and threw her arms around my neck.

"Yes Mike, you have answered my question. You left no doubt about how you feel about me."

"I knew that something was bothering you. The clue was that I gave you ice cream and you didn't immediately reach for a spoon. That's when I knew that something wasn't right."

"Oh shut up and bring me a spoon"

"Yes dear."

"Mike, there is something else I've been thinking about. How do you feel about my daughter and me relocating here? I could transfer and complete my last year of law school here at Boalt Hall at Cal. That way we could be together."

"Wow... I was not expecting that one. What about your daughter? Her moving here would mean that she would be uprooted and would have to make all new friends. That could be very stressful for a kid; don't you think?"

"Actually, the idea of moving to California was her idea. That's why she asks you so many questions when you come to visit. Every time you leave she asks to leave with you. She would love it. Oh by the way. She loves you too."

"What?"

"You heard what I said. She told me so. Michelle has never really gotten to know her biological father and you are the only man I have dated that I have allowed to get emotionally close to her. I didn't even allow my other boyfriends to meet her. She likes talking to you and enjoys the way you help her with her homework and little things like that. She thinks that you are some kind of genius. The thing is, that she does not know how to respond to you. She cried the last time you left Seattle because she misses the attention that you have shown her. She has never gotten attention from a man before. I just thought that you should know."

"Wow... I had no idea. I am nice to Michelle because she is such a sweetheart. I enjoy spending time with both of you. Nothing makes me feel better than putting smiles on my girl's faces. And as far as you moving to California, it may be good idea. It may even be a better idea for me to move to Seattle. I can easily find a job. There's no rush. We'll talk about it more later. Oh... and here's a bit of advice. Any time you make a big proposal like the one you just made, you'll get more traction if you wear that little red teddy that I like so much. I'm just keepin it real."

"Yeah, real perverted."

John's wedding was beautiful if you consider not the fact that the groom and all of the groomsmen were hung over. John's new wife was lovely and a twelve year veteran of the Oakland Police dept. I often teased John about marrying a cop. That's way too many guns in the house.

I told him to make sure he doesn't make her mad or if he does, he should make sure that he is either a better shot than she is or a faster runner.

John and Denise had booked a seven day Caribbean honeymoon cruise that originated in Florida. His flight departed that Sunday night at 8:40PM. Since Remy's flight was within an hour of that time. I drove both of them to the airport.

I hated to see Remy go. I hoped that one day soon such farewells wouldn't be necessary.

Over the next six months or so, Remy and I talked daily on the phone producing huge phone bills. We often discussed the possibility of one of us moving. We finally decided that my moving to Seattle would be more feasible, but the move would have to be put off for a few months so that I could save money.

Remy thought the move should be sooner than later. She said that she had more than enough money to support us until I found employment. I refused.

I didn't know what it felt like to have a woman take care of me and I wasn't interested in finding out. I had always thought that men that leeched off of women were less than men. I could not bring myself to do that, not even for a short period of time.

I was proud of the fact that I had accumulated five months sober. So proud was I that I came to believe that I was cured from my addiction. After all, I hadn't heard from my inner addict in months. I had few urges or cravings. I had begun rebuilding my life and repairing the wreckage that I had caused by living irresponsibly.

My presumption of being cured could not have been more wrong.

ADDICTION IS AN INSIDIOUS, SUBTLE AND MENACING ENEMY OF LIFE.

The addict within will lay in wait for years if necessary for the first opportunity to reappear and finish what he had started. That's why there were people with thirty years or more clean at those AA meetings.

The addict is patient, he is a predator and he is a liar.

He went out of his way to convince me that everything was alright. He convinced me that I no longer needed to go to those dam 12 step meetings while filling my mind with negative images of those that attended.

My inner addict caused me to lie to myself. I was in a state of denial. There is an acronym for the word denial.

D.E.N.I.A.L

DON'T EVEN (K)NOW I AM LYING

I stopped doing the things I did when I became sober. I thought that I could resume a "normal" life, but I didn't even know that I was lying to myself. I was in denial. I did not realize that I am not normal. I am sick. I am an addict.

It was an unusually warm afternoon even for mid August. My apartment was oriented such that the hot afternoon sun beamed unabatedly through my living room and bedroom windows causing my living space to bake like an oven.

It was one of those rare days that I was off work from both my jobs. Remy had called before leaving for school to tell me that she loved me. That made me feel good, but it did not ease the feeling of loneliness that I had been experiencing for the last week or so.

AN ADDICT WHO IS ALONE IS IN BAD COMPANY.

Alcoholcs Anonymous

Though I was lonely, I had no thoughts of getting high. None. Absolutely none. My inner addict had other plans however. What ensued was the strangest thing that has ever happened to me.

Without thinking, I stood up and started walking toward the door. I had absolutely no control of my legs but I knew that I was on my way to buy crack. I tried to stop walking but my attempts were unsuccessful. I walked seven blocks fighting all the way.

I tried grabbing a tree in order to stop my forward momentum, but obviously my legs had convinced my arms that they too needed to get high. After releasing the tree, I continued on this trek. I felt that I was a passenger and non participating observer in my own body.

My arms, now a slave to my legs, reached into my pocket and removed a twenty dollar bill and bought a rock from the crack man. Legs then walked to the liquor store and I bought a pipe and lighter.

Once back home and totally disgusted with myself, I placed the rock on the kitchen table. I sat there and stared at it for about thirty minutes.

I remembered all the wreckage I had allowed it to cause in my life. I tried to recall everything that I learned in Sally.

Control of my legs and arms had been returned to me. My inner addict knows the rules. He could do everything but make me take the first hit. It was up to me to make the next move. My inner addict had set me up.

YOU CAN LEAD A HORSE TO WATER, BUT YOU CAN'T MAKE HIM DRINK

All of the controls and safeguards that I placed on my life to make sure that I never reach this point again were now off. I spent all evening and night getting high. When I woke up the next day, I prayed that God would forgive me and give me the strength to face that day without using. I got dressed and went to work.

Several weeks later my boss called me into his office and informed me that the company was conducting blood pressure screenings of all employees. I had not had my blood pressure checked in years even though I was aware that hypertension ran in my family.

The nurse was shocked after taking my pressure. She told me that my blood pressure was so high that I was a likely candidate for a stroke. She said that she had rarely seen numbers as high as mine and that I should see my doctor as soon as I could.

I made an appointment that day for the following week. The doctor confirmed that my blood pressure was very high. He prescribed medication and told me that if I took the medicine everyday for the rest of my life, my pressure would be in normal range and I would be Okay.

The thought of dying scared me. Cocaine raises blood pressure. My blood pressure was off the chart without cocaine.

YOU ARE EITHER BUSY
WORKING ON YOU RECOVERY
OR YOU ARE BUSY WORKING
ON YOUR RELAPSE

8

SEATTLE

Of all the jobs or tasks that we human beings get to accomplish, packing and moving has got to be the worst. There is no part of this duty that I find stimulating. From the boxing, wrapping, and cleaning, to the loading, storing and lifting. It's all bad.

I rented a storage locker to store the stuff that I wasn't taking with me. I loaded everything else into my truck then hit the road to Seattle.

I had never driven through Northern California, Oregon and Washington State before. It rains so much in the Pacific Northwest that most of the terrain and hillsides were a lush shade of green.

It started raining once I arrived in Portland. The rain turned into a slushy wet snow once I crossed the Washington State line.

I couldn't wait to get to Seattle to see my baby. I had painstakingly managed to stay clean the last five weeks that I was in Oakland. I also regularly attended 12 step meetings. I still harbored apprehension concerning the move. I attributed it to the fear of the unknown. I love acronyms.

F.E.A.R.

FALSE EXPECTATIONS APPEARING REAL

OR

FORGET EVERYTHING AND RUN

When I pulled into Remy's driveway and looked towards Remy's home, I noticed that the curtains in the living room had moved as if someone was peeking through them. I knocked at the door. Remy flung the door open and pulled me inside. He house was lit with the dim glow of candlelight and she was wearing that little red teddy that I like so much. She filled it nicely.

I heard the sound of water running in her tub and I smelled the appetizing aroma of dinner cooking in the kitchen.

Remy handed me a small gift wrapped box with a blue ribbon on it. I opened it and inside I found the door key and garage door opener.

Suddenly, that feeling of fear and apprehension had disappeared, replaced by feelings of affection and love. I felt as if I were welcome.

Tired from my long trip, I stepped into the bubble bath that Remy had prepared for me. Within ten minutes I was asleep.

I was awakened by Remy's soft warm body next to mine in this ocean of bubbles.. Her expressive eyes met mine as we passionately connected in a frenzy of pleasure and love making.

Obviously, judging by the way she responded to me, she thought that I was bowl of banana cream ice cream. Too exhausted to eat the dinner Remy so diligently prepared, we slept until daybreak.

In the morning, I rolled out of bed as Remy slept. I prepared a breakfast consisting of beef sausage and cheese omelets, toast, coffee and orange juice.

I placed this meal on a tray and carried it into the bedroom just as Remy opened her eyes.

"Oh... thank you baby. You are so sweet."

"Yea... I get that a lot. And I figured that after such an exhausting night like the one you had last night, you would be in no condition to get up, let alone cook this morning."

"I see that I'm gonna have to deflate that ego of yours.

"I removed the tray from her lap."

"Give me my food you horny crazy man. I'm hungry", she said as she laughed.

"What are your plans for today?"

"I have to do some research for a moot court that's taking place tomorrow. I should be home by two o'clock. I also have to pick up Michelle from school. She spent last night at my sisters house. What's on your agenda?"

"I am going to update my resume and then use your computer to post it online."

"My computer? You mean our computer. I want you to feel comfortable in knowing that everything in this house is ours."

"Thank you sweetie. I needed to hear you say that. I love you very much. Now get out of my bed and go to school. I can pick up Michelle from school if you want me to. What do you want to do for dinner?"

"Remember, last night's dinner is still in the refrigerator. Maybe I'll give you a chance to eat it tonight."

"If that's the case, then I'll be lucky if last nights dinner is still in the refrigerator tomorrow. I love you. Have a good day. Can't wait to put my hands on you again."

"Is sex the only thing that you think about?"

"Yes. You say that like that's a bad thing. Besides I haven't seen you in weeks. I have a lot of catching up to do. Oh...by the way, I think that after picking up Michelle from school, I'll take her for ice cream. Is that okay."

"Sure, she would love that. Just don't share with her the information I told you about her."

After eating Remy showered, dressed, then left for school.

I felt good about my decision to relocate to Seattle. I saw a bright future with Remy. It was if my prayers were answered and God had sent someone to fill the void that was left in my life after the accident that took the life of my wife and son.

Remy's brother gave me information about employment with the Port of Seattle through ILWU Local 21. He told me that all I would have to do is show up at 6:00AM each morning until, based on seniority, I'm sent out on a job with the port. I would then work there the rest of the month, then report back to the union hall again on the first of the following month and repeat the process.

I took his advice and showed up on the third of the month. I reported and waited each day until I was sent out on the eleventh of the month to a warehouse in Renton, Washington. My job was to fill containers with mostly toys for shipment to overseas markets.

I had never operated a fork lift, but by the second week I was a pro at it.

Within three months I had obtained a second job unloading rail cars filled with boxes of frozen chicken feet for shipment to Asian countries.

This job was physically draining because hundreds of sixty pound boxes had to be lifted by hand and thrown from the train.

Because the temperature in the rail cars were maintained below freezing, several layers of clothing were required to be worn as we worked in the falling snow and cold weather of Seattle.

I gained twenty pounds of muscle and flaunted a nice six pack after working there for only a month.

I quit the rail car unloading job after a month when I learned of a position with a security company.

My job there was to secure a large apartment complex whose owner was evicting all tenants in order that he may remodel the units.

The transmission on my truck had been slipping for the last several days. It finally gave out on me on my way to work one day so Remy and I shared her car. Remy was a good sport about it. I would take her to school every morning and pick her up in the afternoons or evenings.

I know that a crack addict cannot get high if he doesn't take that first hit. The same is true for other types of addictions besides drugs. For example, an alcoholic cannot get drunk if he doesn't take his first drink. The same is true for cigarettes, food, gambling or any other addiction.

It is also true that the addict is only responsible for that first hit, drink, smoke, bet or other devise. After the first one, the addict is on automatic pilot.

He is unable to control the outcome of his actions even though he is a participant in that outcome. He will continue the reckless or life threatening behavior until something happens to stop him. A drug addict or gambler will run out of money or die. A cigarette smoker will develop lung cancer or die of heart disease.

Sir Isaac Newton unwittingly proved this point when he developed his first law of motion:

AN OBJECT IN MOTION TENDS TO REMAIN IN MOTION UNLESS AN EXTERNAL FORCE IS APPLIED TO IT.

Newton's first law of motion

Mr. Newton probably had not considered that his law of motion had any implications beyond physics. But when the addict in me is released, I am powerless to stop him. Some external force must be utilized to bring me back to my rational mind.

AN ADDICT ON DRUGS TENDS TO REMAIN ON DRUGS UNTIL AN OUTSIDE FORCE IS APPLIED TO HIS LIFE

Mike's first law of destruction

The external forces that many addicts that have achieved long term sobriety apply in their lives are the spiritual principals set forth in twelve step programs. It is the belief that a higher power can restore us to sanity.

It is a belief in something larger than ourselves. In fact six of the twelve steps mention God by name.

IT IS IMPERATIVE THAT THE ADDICT TAKES WHATEVER MEASURES AVAILABLE TO HIM TO AVOID TAKING THE FIRST HIT, FIX, DRINK, SMOKE, BET OR OTHER DEVISE.

The cunning nature of the addict within cannot be understated. He assumes that if you are clean long enough, one day you will forget that he is there.

The addict is very patient. While he waits, he is becoming stronger. He is doing push-ups in your head while waiting for his chance to show himself and destroy your life all over again.

Such was the case one Sunday night when a new and improved, Arnold Schwarzenegger sized version of my addict appeared with a vengeance.

Like a polar bear that has hibernated all winter, he was awake and hungry after his long slumber and was ready to open a can of whupass on me all over again.

I was working my security job when a young lady called the security office complaining of someone breaking into a vacant apartment. I arrived and found a man and woman smoking crack. They became spooked when they saw me; both ran past me and out of the door leaving their drugs and paraphernalia behind on the kitchen counter.

There were, at the time, lots of options that I could have chosen that would have guaranteed a positive outcome. I could have flushed the drug down the toilet, threw it out of the window or just left it there.

My decision to smoke the drug was made with indifference toward the consequences. The beast was awake, active and took no prisoners.

My decision to take that first hit set in motion a series of events that would ultimately ruin the relationship that took me many months to build.

TO A DRUG ADDICT OR ALCOHOLIC THE ONLY IMPORTANT HIT OR DRINK IS THE NEXT ONE.

Over the next several weeks, my using continued and Remy began noticing changes in my personality. When she asked me about it, I simply dismissed her accusations as figments of her imagination. I would also explain away the fact that money was missing and that I was frequently late picking her up from school.

The more I got high, the stronger my addict grew. I was powerless to do anything about it.

One payday, I found myself in a crack house. I had dropped Remy off at school before picking up my check. I ended up staying in that house for two days until my entire paycheck was gone.

The problem was that I had not called Remy and I had her car, which meant that she was stranded and could not get to school. I faced going home with great trepidation.

I had made up my mind that I was going to tell Remy about my past and come clean concerning my addiction.

"Hello Remy"

"Mike, where have you been? I've called the police and reported you missing. I've been worried sick about you. I thought that you had been involved in an accident or something. Where were you?"

"Remy let's sit down. I need to talk to you."

"I don't want to sit down. I want to know where you were."

"OK. There is something that you don't know about me. I am an addict. I've been in recovery for the past year or so. I relapsed a few weeks ago. I have been getting high for the last two days. I think that you should know this."

"You mean to tell me that I've been worried sick about you, calling hospitals, and you were somewhere getting high? What are you addicted to?"

"Crack."

"You had my car for two days. I had to take the bus to school and you were hold up somewhere smoking crack! You should have told me about this a long time ago."

"You are right. I should have told you a long time ago. All that I can do now is tell you how sorry I am and ask you to forgive me."

"I can't talk to you right now. I need some time and space. Give me my car keys."

Remy left that day and spent the weekend at her sister's house. When she returned, she told me that if I were to use one more time our relationship would be over and I would have to move out. However, this would not be the final word on the incident.

While on my security job the following Monday, Remy drove up to the security booth I occupied and told me that she had reconsidered. She said that she did not think it safe to have me in the same house as her daughter anymore because I was on drugs.

She had packed my belongings in my two suitcases which she removed from her trunk and presented to me. That was the last time that I saw Remy.

Suddenly, life jumped up and bit me in the ass. I found myself, on this job with two suit cases containing all my worldly possessions, in this city where I knew almost no one, I had no money, no car, no place to live, nowhere to go and an addict within that was determined to make my life miserable.

AN ADDICT WHO IS ALONE IS IN BAD COMPANY

I never faulted Remy for the decision that I forced her to make. I think that any mother would have made the same decision out of concern for her kid.

However this breakup was especially hard for me because I loved Remy so much. I experienced a sense of loss that I only had to face once before in my life. Remy, Michelle and I had become a family. Now I felt that I was loosing another family.

I had no time to grieve the loss because I had more pertinent problems to resolve. Like where was I going to live and how was I going to pay for it.

I told the owner of the security company of my plight. He told me that I could stay in one of the vacant apartments of this sprawling property for free until I found a place.

The next day while at my second job, I told the business owner what had happened. He told me that he had an older Volvo that was collecting dust in his garage. He gave me the car and charged me not.

The owner of the security company had more good news for me. He told me that the company had a contract with a very large condominium complex in Renton, WA. He told me that he had spoken to the management office about me and they were willing to

---

rent a two bedroom luxury condo to me for less than half the market rate and they would waive the deposits.

Suddenly all my lemons had become lemonade. However, as evident of my self destructive behavior, I did my best to try to convert that lemonade back into lemons.

My using continued to increase. I lost the Port of Seattle job because of a dirty drug test. Then I fell two months behind on my rent and eventually failed to show up at the security job. I was eventually evicted from the condo.

Once again broke, Jobless and homeless on the streets of Seattle, I lived in my Volvo. Within a few weeks I entered a State of Washington sponsored drug program called Cedar Hills.

Desperate for solutions to my situation and with a strong desire to reconcile my relationship with Remy, I took the program quite seriously.

Cedar Hills was very different from Sally. It is nestled in the hills above Seattle and was not a working program so more time was devoted to recovery. Twelve step programs were stressed. We were in meetings or groups from 9AM till 4PM on most days.

I remember watching a nature special a few years ago. There were these very small baitfish whose method of protection against predators involved swimming in very large schools, some the size of football fields.

This huge blob, at the hint of a threat would change directions in the blink of an eye. In fact, because of this schooling habit, they are incapable of living solitary lives. They would do everything in schools including eating and mating.

Well, along came a school of dolphins trolling for a meal. The dolphins broke the large school of baitfish into several manageable groups.

The dolphins also forced the baitfish upwards in order to trap them against the surface of the water. The dolphins then took turns diving into the schools of baitfish and gorging themselves until every baitfish in the blob was gone.

I couldn't help but to feel sorry for the little baitfish. They were locked into their habits and behaviors and could not change. The protection of the school had become their downfall.

While watching this baitfish slaughter in HD, I remember thinking that if I were one of those baitfish, I would take my chances and stray from the flock and strike out on my own while the dolphins were preoccupied with eating all of my buddies.

After all, self preservation is the first law of nature. That way at least I would have a chance at survival.

I think it curious that we human beings at times become caught up in herding behavior. Addicts have raised this character defect to an art form.

We should be able to see that if we don't make changes in our lives that the result will be gloom and doom.

But we continue our destructive ways because it seems natural to do so. We surround ourselves with people with the same self destructive habits and defects of character. We have been doing the same things for so long, just like the baitfish; it's the only thing we know, so we follow without thinking.

It is hard to venture out on your own. Just ask the baitfish.

To acquire independence we have to:

1. CONVINCE OURSELVES THAT REMAINING WITH THE PACK WILL EVENTUALLY CAUSE US TO LOOSE OUR LIVES.

2. DECIDE THAT OUR LIVES ARE WORTH SAVING.

3. TAKE ACTION BEFORE IT'S TOO LATE

The clock is ticking. I used mind and mood altering substances for years, but I always knew in the back of my mind that there come a day that I would no longer have the need or desire to get high.

The problem was that the thoughts were in the back of my mind. Those thoughts needed to be brought up to the front of my mind where they could do some good, and no-one could do that for me but me.

I needed incentives in my daily life because there are always tomorrows. There are 365 tomorrows each year and they seem to fly by way too fast when I waste them getting loaded.

I'm sure that many of the baitfish in the huge school thought that they might survive the dolphin onslaught just for today. But they didn't, and they died.

Some probably figured that they just weren't ready to leave the group. They were wrong and they died. One may have thought that because he was so deep in the pack that the dolphins would be full by the time they got to him. May he rest in peace.

The key is that I must make a decision everyday that my desire for a good life free of bad habits must remain first and foremost in my mind.

Each day that I awake (luckily I've awakened everyday so far) I thank God for allowing me so many days of sobriety and I ask that this blessing be extended for one more day. Then I'm up and ready for a new day.

These are some of the lessons that I have learned during the three month Cedar Hill Program. After graduating from the program, I was placed in transitional housing that was owned by a large corporation that had such housing and hotels all over the Seattle area.

The housing offered a safe place for me to live. I had my own room and everyone in the home shared the kitchen and bathroom. There were chores that needed to be done everyday and a midnight curfew. Most importantly, the addict that dwelled within me was in remission. I intended to keep him that way.

I was fortunate enough to live two blocks from a twelve step fellowship hall. I spent more time there than I spent at home. I was there waiting at the door at seven o'clock in the morning. I made coffee for that early morning meeting and attended every meeting every day. Between meetings I played dominos with the other members and did service work such as sweeping and cleaning.

The fact was that I was afraid to leave the hall. I did not think that I was ready to face life on life's terms outside of the hall so fellowshipping with other recovering addicts became my higher power. It worked too. I made lots of friends and the meetings were inspirational.

I had heard that another transition house that was owned by the company that owned the one that I lived was looking for a house manager. House managers received a significant rent discount, so I was quick to apply.

After a week or so, I received a call from Sandy, who was the office manager. Sandy told me that the house manager position was filled but she had reviewed my resume and thought that I would be a good fit for the Heath Hotel.

The Heath was a 12 story hotel in downtown Seattle that catered to mostly low end travelers and tourist. The hotel had just been renovated and was in need of an assistant hotel director.

I thought the chances of my getting this job were less than zero. I applied the next day and was hired within a week.

The salary was moderate, but the money went a long way because I was required to live in one of the rooms on the property therefore I paid no rent. I also ate meals in the hotel's restaurant three times daily for free so I did not have to buy food. I also had full use of the hotel's truck so I did not have to drive my now malfunctioning Volvo.

My primary responsibilities were to make sure that every guest had paid their rent on time or if not promptly evict them. I also had to make sure that the rooms were clean and I managed all hotel employees.

Normally, this would be an ideal opportunity for someone trying to get established in a strange city. However, the Heath was located in a not so good part of downtown Seattle.

Running the hotel required a great deal of time and energy which left very little time to work on me and my recovery. I thought that I could bury myself into my work the way I buried myself into my work at the fellowship hall. All I managed to do was to bury myself. Within a month I was getting high again.

In retrospect, I realize that it was too soon for me to work that job. I had only been sober for four months. I was not yet secure enough in my sobriety to handle such a huge responsibility.

Some of the employees had suspected that I had been getting loaded so they went to the hotel director who drug tested me. The drug test was dirty. My boss told me that I would have to be off the property in three days.

Losing this job was traumatic for me. I felt that I had squandered all of God's gifts. While employed, I had access to food, clothing, shelter, a vehicle, and income.

Upon losing the job, I was homeless, foodless, broke, and had no transportation.

I slept in the non- working Volvo for a while until the Volvo and my carpet cleaning equipment were towed by the Seattle police.

THE ADDICT THAT DWELLED WITHIN ME WAS OUT OF CONTROL. MY SENSE OF PURPOSE WAS LOST. I REGULARLY DID THINGS THAT I USED TO ARREST PEOPLE FOR.

I ran the streets of Seattle, hustling money in order to feed my addiction and for food and shelter.

A homeless guy had taught me a hustle which involved stealing small items from local stores and supermarkets, then either selling them or returning them to the store for refunds. After a while I became good at doing it.

I graduated to stealing larger items from department stores and quality cuts of steaks from supermarkets. I had regular customers that would purchase the merchandise from me for half the marked price.

I had decided that I needed to move back to California. I felt apprehensive about leaving Seattle because I felt that there were still things unresolved between Remy and me. I knew that she still had strong feelings for me, but I knew that as long as I continued to use cocaine, there would be no hope of restoring the special <u>bonds</u> that we once shared. I will always love Rene.

I managed to hustle several hundred dollars and used some of it to purchase a ticket and flew back to Oakland. By this time, my addict was a monster. It was like, the addict was in control and I was in the background watching him place my life and freedom at risk.

9

HITTING
BOTTOM

I did not care about anything or anyone outside of getting high. I cared not about what I had to do or who I had to hurt to get drugs. My waking hours were spent thinking of nothing but smoking crack and I was developing a taste for alcohol. I rented a room at an East Oakland hotel because it was known for drugs and prostitution.

My weight had dropped from 225 lbs to 195 lbs. and I had stopped taking my high blood pressure medication. As much as I wanted to stop smoking crack, I could not bring myself to doing it.

I used the same hustles that I had perfected in Seattle. I noticed that stores in Oakland employed more security guards than in the Seattle area. Still I managed to be successful at my illegal activities. But I felt that I was stuck in a deep hole and was unable to get out.

THERE WAS ONCE AN ADDICT STUCK IN A DEEP HOLE. A DOCTOR CAME ALONG AND SAW THE MAN DOWN IN THE HOLE. THE MAN EXPLAINED HIS SITUATION TO THE DOCTOR AND THE DOCTOR WROTE OUT A PRESCRIPTION, THREW IT DOWN TO THE MAN IN THE HOLE AND WALKED AWAY. SOON, A PRIEST WALKED BY AND NOTICED THE MAN DOWN IN THE HOLE. WHEN THE MAN ASKED THE PRIEST FOR HELP, THE PRIEST WROTE OUT A PRAYER, THREW IT DOWN TO THE MAN AND WALKED AWAY. A RECOVERING ADDICT THEN CAME ALONG AND AFTER HEARING OF THE MAN'S PLIGHT, JUMPED INTO THE HOLE WITH THE ADDICT. THE ADDICT SAID, "WHAT ARE YOU DOING. NOW WE ARE BOTH STUCK. WE'LL NEVER GET OUT OF HERE." THE RECOVERING ADDICT THEN SAID, "IT'S OK. I'VE BEEN DOWN HERE BEFORE AND I KNOW THE WAY OUT. FOLLOW ME."

Sometimes God sends angels.

It was a very warm day in Oakland and I was walking to no where in particular sweating like a pig when I noticed a newer Chevy Blazer with a flat tire parked on the oposite side of the street. The owner had just opened the trunk and had removed the jack.

Seeing this as an opportunity to make a few dollars to buy some drugs, I approached him and asked if he needed my help.

The older gentleman looked at me for a few seconds, and then told me that he would give me a few dollars if I were to help him.

As we changed the tire, he seemed to take an interest in my personal life. He asked questions about my work and marriage life. Then he said something that really shocked me.

"How long you been smoking that shit?"

"What makes you think I smoke anything?"

"You are right, I'm sorry sir. I should not assume."

After a long pause I said, "On and off for about seven years. I feel like I'm stuck in a deep hole."

"It's Ok. I've been down there before and I know the way out. After I fix this tire I'm going to an AA meeting. You would be doing me a favor if you were to go with me. You see... helping fellow addicts keeps me sober. So will you help me out?"

I didn't really want to go. I wanted to go to the dope man and buy a piece of crack. But something inside of me convinced me to go with the old fellow. I think that it was my rational mind trying to dig himself out of the grave of disgrace of which I had buried him.

My new friend raised his hand in the meeting in order to share his experience, strength and hope. I learned that his name was Ralph R. and he had been sober from alcohol for the past 26 years.

I found Ralph to be an extremely intelligent person and I learned a great deal from him that day.

After the meeting, Ralph took me to dinner at a crowded barbeque house where my education continued.

H.A.L.T

AN ADDICT SHOULD NEVER GET TOO H.UNGRY A.NGRY L.ONELY OR T.IRED

"It is strange that you should mention that Ralph. I vividly remember being angry at my self after my fiancé died. I was also angry at God for taking her away from me. I was also very lonely during that time. I isolated myself from my friends, family, employees and people in general. I worked from home and sometimes didn't leave my house for weeks.

"Do you think that your state of mind caused you to start using"

"Well it certainly didn't help. How do I stop using?"

"Well, I have some good news and some bad news. The bad news is that there is not a single thing that you can do to stop getting high. The good news is that there are twelve things that you can do to stop getting high. They are...

1. WE ADMITTED WE WERE POWERLESS OVER OUR ADDICTION- THAT OUR LIVES HAD BECOME UNMANAGEABLE.

2. WE CAME TO BELIEVE THAT A POWER GREATER THAN OURSELVES COULD RESTORE US TO SANITY.

3. WE MADE A DECISION TO TURN OUR WILL AND OUR LIVES OVER TO THE CARE OF GOD AS WE UNDERSTAND GOD.

4. WE MADE A SEARCHING AND FEARLESS MORAL INVENTORY OF OURSELVES.

5. WE ADMITTED TO GOD, TO OURSELVES AND TO ANOTHER HUMAN BEING THE EXACT NATURE OF OUR WRONGS.

6. WE WERE ENTIRELY READY TO HAVE GOD REMOVE ALL THESE DEFECTS OF CHARACTER

7. WE HUMBLY ASKED HIM TO REMOVE OUR SHORTCOMINGS.

8. WE MADE A LIST OF ALL PERSONS WE HAD HARMED, AND BECAME WILLING TO MAKE AMENDS TO THEM ALL.

9. WE MADE DIRECT AMENDS TO SUCH PEOPLE WHEREVER POSSIBLE, EXCEPT WHEN TO DO SO WOULD INJURE THEM OR OTHERS.

10. WE CONTINUED TO TAKE PERSONAL INVENTORY AND WHEN WE WERE WRONG PROMPTLY ADMITTED IT

11. WE SOUGHT THROUGH PRAYER AND MEDITATION TO IMPROVE CONTACT WITH GOD, PRAYING ONLY FOR KNOWLEDGE OF GOD'S WILL FOR US AND THE POWER TO CARRY THAT OUT

12. HAVING HAD A SPIRITUAL AWAKENING AS A RESULT OF THESE STEPS, WE TRIED TO CARRY THIS MESSAGE TO OTHER ADDICTS, AND TO PRACTICE THESE PRINCIPLES IN ALL OUR AFFAIRS.

-
alcoholic anonymous

I listened to Ralph recite the twelve steps as if it was my first time hearing them. I had heard them recited and had read them many times before, but they had never sunken into my subconscious as they did when recited by Ralph.

"Mike have you ever worked the steps?"

"No. I tried to work them by myself once. It didn't work out so well. I think that I need some help. Will you help me?"

"Sure; but you have to be ready. Do you think that you are ready?"

"No I don't. Not right now. I don't think that I could remain sober in my current living environment."

"I'll give you my phone number. Call me any time. Even if you just want to talk."

Ralph dropped me off at the hotel. As I got out of his truck, Ralph reached into his pocket and gave me a ten dollar bill. I had forgotten that he had not paid me for helping him to change the tire.

"You have been so kind to me that I feel bad about taking your money. But I do need it, so thank you very much."

"Just promise me that you won't buy drugs with it."

"You have my word on that. You also have my word that I will call you. I have never had a sponsor before. I'll call you soon. I promise that I will call when I'm ready."

Now I would love to say that I saved the money that Ralph gave me, but the truth is that I walked away from Ralph's truck and walked directly to the dope man.

I continued living the street life and smoking and drinking everyday. I have no idea how and don't know when I picked up a cigarette habit. But I did and before long, I was up to a pack per day.

I soon fell into the trap that tobacco companies use of selling two packs for the price of one. Before long I was smoking two packs per day.

Shoplifting had become a way of life for me. I spent most of my days running in and out of stores taking their stuff.

My lucky streak ran out when I was arrested by an undercover security officer after stuffing three huge packs of beef steaks down my pants and walking out of the door. For the first time in my life I was in custody and handcuffed.

I sat in the rear of the store waiting for the Oakland police officer to arrive to take me to jail. I couldn't help but to feel sorry for myself for my fall from grace.

I heard the squelch of a police radio before seeing the officer walk through the swinging doors.

"Oh shit." I said out loud as I looked into the face of the officer. There were more that six hundred officers on the Oakland police department and I get to be arrested by one of my best friends.

John did not recognize me at first because I had lost so much weight and I looked so much like a crack head.

"What's up John?"

John looked at me curiously. "Do I know you sir?"

"Yes, you know me very well."

"Mike. Mike this can't be you. Mike, what the hell are you doing? I haven't heard from you in a long time. Now I know why. Are you smoking that shit. You don't have to answer that. I can tell by just looking at you."

Since this was my first offense and I had ID, John cited me and gave me a court date, so I was spared the embarrassment of being transported to jail. But I was not released before I was verbally chastised for more than an hour while sitting in the back of John's police car.

I had come full circle. From arrester to arrestee.

I went back to my room feeling about six inches tall. I conducted a complete evaluation of my life and the results made me feel even smaller.

I once owned a nice home. Now I am lucky if I can hustle up enough money to pay the $35 per day rent for a filthy, roach infested room that's surrounded by dope fiends and prostitutes.

I once had nice cars, then I had none. At one time I routinely carried 225 lbs. on my 6'3" frame. At one time I had good jobs and a business. Today, I was arrested for stealing meat to sell in order to buy crack. My weight was about 180 lbs.

Most of all, I lost my dignity and self respect. I routinely did things I never would have before imagined doing.

After a couple hours of self loathing, I stood and walked toward the bathroom. As I walked I passed a small mirror in the hall, I was startled by the reflection of another person in my room.

I frantically looked behind me to see who the unauthorized person was. There was no one there.

I again looked in the mirror and saw no-one but myself.

It was then that I realized that there was no other person in the room. The drugs that I so routinely placed in my body had such a devastating affect on my

THE DOPELESS HOPE FIEND

appearence that I recognized the person staring back at me in the mirror not.

I immediately removed my wallet from my left rear pocket and removed a match book cover with a phone number written on it.

I hastily walked to the phone booth that was located under an awning at the entrance of the hotel and dialed the seven digits.

"Hello Ralph, this is Mike. I'm ready!"

"Where are you?"

"I'm at my room."

"I'm on my way."

Ralph was there within twenty minutes. He took me to an AA meeting at the In-Between Fellowship Hall, then out for a cup of coffee.

"Mike, wasn't that a good meeting? In AA, they tell us that when you feel that you want to use, get to a meeting. If your ass falls off, pick your ass up and take it to the meeting with you and place your ass on the chair right next to you. It took a lot of courage for you to make that phone call."

"I don't think so. In fact I thought that it was pretty cowardly of me. I had no other place to go. I was afraid that if I continued on this path that I wouldn't live to see too many more sunrises. My life and my addiction are unmanageable and I am out of control. I didn't know where to turn. So I called you."

"Thanks for calling. I told you. Helping other addicts keeps me sober. Years ago when I really struggled, I found it helpful to get out of myself and help someone else. It's hard to feel sorry for yourself when you are doing something of good for someone else. In AA, they call what you are having right now, a moment of clarity. So listen to your heart. Put that addict in your back pocket. Now... what do you want to do?"

"I need to get off the streets. I'm thinking about getting in a program."

"A friend of mine is a pastor at The Missionary Church in Berkeley which has a treatment program in Oakland. I've heard nothing but good things about the program. Do you want to check it out?"

"Yes I do. Will they take me in tonight?"

"There's only one way to find out."

Ralph drove me back to my room where I gathered my things and then took me to the residence where the program is housed.

The house is a well maintained three story Victorian in West Oakland. Ralph and I walked up to the door and knocked. A short man with glasses and the voice of a preacher answered and told that his name was Goody.

Goody was a graduate of the program and was currently the managing director. I explained to him that I needed help.

GOD IS ALWAYS THERE WHEN YOU NEED HIM

Goody gave a tour of the residence and introduced me to the residents. I was treated as if I were one of the family. Goody showed me to my bunk and explained to me that because I was new, I would be allowed to sleep all day the following day. I thanked God for that. I had been up for two days smoking crack and stealing.

I thanked Ralph for his patience and understanding as I shook his hand.

I remember thinking as my friend Ralph drove away that when I have enough sobriety behind me, I'm going help other addicts to stay clean. But first I needed to focus on me.

I slept for two days straight. I didn't even wake up for meals. The third day, I met Pastor Choyce who was the pastor of the church and the person whom had envisioned the men's treatment program as part of his ministry years prior. Pastor Choyce seemed to be an extremely intelligent and caring man.

Cocaine is an inexplicable and devious drug. It is very easy to fall into the trap of smoking it everyday, and if you do so, your mind will tell you that you need to smoke it everyday. So you get involved in this repeating loop that will continue until you do something to interrupt the loop.

IF YOU THINK YOU CAN OR IF YOU THINK YOU CAN'T, YOU'RE PROBABLY RIGHT.

When the loop is interrupted, you can go long periods of time without using. But you still crave it. The longer you stay away from it, the weaker the cravings get. But they never go away totally, which is why you have to stay on top of it and maintain a program of long term sobriety so that when your addict returns and again wants to take over, you will know what steps to take to ward off the attack.

Remember, while you are sober your addict is in your brain doing push-ups.

Missionary's program wasn't nearly as rigorous as the Salvation Army or Cedar Hills programs. I found that to be refreshing. I had lots of time for independent studies and reading. And since it was a Christian program, I had lots of time and resources to start to reconcile my strained relationship with God.

Each day would start off the same way. Everyone in the house would wake up at 5 AM, gather in the large dining area on the first floor and sing praise and worship songs. Breakfast was prepared at 7 AM then everyone would get into vans and go to the church for bible studies and group sessions. Usually we were back at the residence by early afternoon.

I befriended two residents while at Missionary. One of them was Al. Al was an addict that seemed to know everything about the bible and was quick to enumerate everyone else's faults.

I think that Al had memorized the bible and would, like a gunslinger and with little provocation, whip out a chapter and verse on you at the blink of an eye. But he was a funny guy and he meant well, so he became one of my best friends.

My other friend was an addict whose name was Kurt. Kurt was 5'9", 250 lbs. and built like a bowling ball. He is an ex-football player who liked to throw his weight around. The extra testosterone made him a very competitive person. He constantly challenged everyone to arm-wrestle, to play dominos or some similar activity.

Unfortunately Kurt was a sore loser. Every time I beat him at dominos, he would get mad and want to wrestle, which would not have been so bad if he was a normal size human being. But wrestling with Kurt was like being attacked by a small rhino with a low center of gravity.

The twelve month program was the best thing that could have happened to me at that time. It gave me a chance to refocus and reorganize my life. However, my stay was cut to four months when Kurt and I decided to accept a job in construction.

The job was offered by a young woman whose name was Beth. Beth owned lots of property in the area including a boarded up house next to the program residence.

Beth was a kind and generous woman. She had given Kurt and me a two bedroom apartment to share while we worked for her. We left the program to take advantage of the opportunity.

I guess the lesson I should have learned in Seattle while working at the Heath did not stick because here I was again taking a job that I was not prepared to take.

Pastor Choyce tried desperately to get us to stay, but my addict lied to me and told me that I was ready to handle the responsibility. In reality my addict wanted nothing more to do recovery and was ready to reemerge.

Within three weeks I had started smoking crack again. Kurt had started shooting heroin again.

NOTHING CHANGES IF NOTHING CHANGES

Alcoholics Anonymous

Kurt soon moved out of the apartment but Beth allowed me to stay there alone.

Before long, I was running a full fledge crack house out of my apartment. All times of the day and night dope fiends in the area would knock at my door and either pay with money or with crack for the opportunity to sit and smoke with me.

After hearing multiple complaints from several neighbors, Beth fired me and told me that I would have to vacate the apartment.

I should have seen this coming from a mile away. It is a repeat of what happened to me in Seattle. They say hind sight is 20/20 but there is no way that such an obvious gaff should have escaped my gaze.

In retrospect, I realize that I did see it coming. I just did not care. Consequences did not matter. I just wanted to get high and I was ready and willing to do whatever that was necessary to make that happen.

Nothing changes if nothing changes. But at that low point in my life, the only thing that I was interested in changing was the brillo in my crack pipe. I was on one. For real. And it nearly cost me my life.

With no where to go and very little money in my pocket to get there, I went to the welfare office and was placed in a shelter that was run by the county. The building was located in East Oakland in a spacious turn of the century renovated office building.

The shelter was like being near ground zero at crack central. It was like being in a state sponsored crack house.

There was a curfew set at 11:00 PM unless you had a job that kept you out later.

I had gotten a job at a Mexican night club in East Oakland as a bouncer. The owner of the club paid me and three other guards cash every night at 2 AM when the club closed, four days per week. With very little supervision at the shelter, it was easy for me to live the self destructive lifestyle of an addict.

After living there for five months, a decision was made by the shelter to not allow residents to work after hours. Not wanting to quit my job, I elected to move from the shelter and into an abandoned and non-working mini van. I also rented hotel rooms when I could afford them.

I lived this way for the next two years. I had been promoted to head of security at the Mexican night club, but I continued living on the street and smoking everyday.

I started stealing again in order to supplement my income. Stealing socks underwear, T-shirts, and tennis shoes were my specialty. I had a growing list of customers that wanted them. Most of them were drug dealers. It *was* convenient that they paid with crack. It eliminated the middleman.

I am convinced that addiction is a disease. Previously, I had dismissed the disease paradigm as psychobabble, but now I get the connection.

Encarta dictionary gives three categories for the word disease and gives the definition of each:

1. MEDICAL CONDITION- A CONDITION IN HUMANS... THAT RESULTS IN PATHOLOGICAL SYMPTOMS AND IS NOT THE RESULT OF PHYSICAL INJURY.

2. SPECIFIC DISORDER- A DISORDER IN HUMANS... WITH RECOGNIZABLE SIGNS.

3. PROBLEM IN SOCIETY- A SERIOUS PROBLEM IN SOCIETY OR WITH A GROUP OF PEOPLE.

All three definitions illustrate what happens to me when I get high. My condition is medical because when the pathogen (mind altering substance) is introduced into my system, symptoms of uncontrollability and self destruction ensues.

My thievery and general anti-social behavior creates a huge problem in society.

The disease of addiction can be compared to other social diseases. A person with an STD can avoid a reoccurrence of the affliction by avoiding sex.

However in most human beings, abstinence is not an option so that person will continue with their destructive sexual behavior risking re-infection.

When a person uses alcohol or drugs, the pleasure centers of the brain becomes hyperactive. So getting high to an addict can be compared to having sex.

Many addicts believe (falsely) that abstinence from alcohol and drugs is not an option, so the addict will continue with his destructive behavior risking death.

If a man knows for a fact that a particular woman has a disease such as AIDS, he may be inclined to avoid her, regardless of how attracted he is to her. She may be physically the perfect woman in every respect for him and posses all the features he finds attractive.

In this case, immediate gratification goes out the window. His focus is on the immediate future and things like visits to the doctor's office or ingesting a regiment of medication. Chances are, he will pass up the opportunity to pleasure himself. He takes pause and considers the consequences of his actions.

The same is not true for the addict. The addict will, without hesitation, rush into the health and life threatening situation as it relates to his drug use. Not once will he consider the consequences of the drink or hit. If he happens to consider the consequences, it'll have no affect on his actions.

Such was the case one evening when I happened to meet a young woman named Charlotte. I told Charlotte that I had money and drugs but no place to go and smoke it.

Charlotte told me that she had a friend who lived in the neighborhood whose home we could sit and smoke. Once we got to the house, I recognized it as a place where several robberies have taken place. But I did not care. I decided to ignore the possible consequences.

After being in the home for about an hour, two gangster types came in and went to the back bedroom. Charlotte told me that the duo were going to rob me and that I should hide my money in the bathroom.

Suspecting that Charlotte was up to no good, I got up and went into the bathroom and pretended that I was hiding money in there.

I happened to be wearing a pair of sweats that had a lining. Through a hole in my pocket I slipped the $250 I had. The money fell to the ankle between the sweats and the lining. I walked back to the living room and sat on the couch.

As soon as I came out of the bathroom, Charlotte went into the bathroom and locked the door. I don't know what she was doing in there, but when she came out, the owner of the house was angry that Charlotte had messed up her bathroom.

Charlotte went to the back bedroom apparently to tell the two robbers that the money wasn't in the bathroom.

The robbery duo then came into the living room. One of them was holding a gun and looking at me.

"Hey man, if you are trying to rob me, you'll just be practicing. I don't know what that broad told you but I have no money." I said.

"Well my brotha, we're gonna have a butt naked party just to be sure. Take it all off."

I stood and took off all of my clothes and gave them to the one not holding the gun. When I gave him the sweatpants, he searched the pockets but his search went nowhere near the ankles where my money was stashed. He then gave my clothes back to me.

The duo were so angry at Charlotte for telling them that I had money, that they took her to the back room and beat and raped her. I heard her screams as I walked away from the home. I felt the protection of God's grace as I walked.

TO THE ADDICT, IMMEDIATE GRATIFICATION TRUMPS NEGATIVE CONSEQUENCES.

It's like the man that enjoys the feeling of being cracked in the head with a hammer, so he picks up a hammer and smacks himself in the cranium. He's rushed to the hospital by ambulance and the doctors meticulously care for his skull. He is bandaged and placed in a room to recover.

Now, the man can't wait to be discharged so that he can get home to his hammer and slap himself in the head with it again.

I remember metaphorically smacking myself in the head with a hammer one day while in a department store. I stuffed several packs of t-shirts, socks and boxer shorts down my pants, and then attempted to walk out of the door. I thought that I had been careful to remove the electronic detection devices from the items but in my haste I missed one of the packages.

All hell broke loose when the door alarm sounded. The security guard sarcastically said that he did not notice that I was pregnant when I walked into the store. I called him every name in the book and a few that hadn't been put in the book yet, then I broke and ran toward the parking lot.

Now, I realized that I was no world class sprinter, but I have always been quick on my feet. This smart ass of a security guard obviously doubled as a super hero because he caught me before I was halfway across the lot.

As I ran, I heard someone yell,"Hey, look at that security guard running after that pregnant guy".

This low budget comedian of a security guard ran along side of me, slowed to match my speed and said, "Nice day for a run isn't it?"

I immediately stop running and started walking back toward the entrance of the store, escorted by the guard.

I felt indifferent to the eyes of the public as I walked back through the store and into the security office. Once there, I was handcuffed and searched revealing the items that I had taken. The security guard filled out his report then called the Oakland police.

While waiting for the police to arrive, I remember being very upset at myself. I had made a promise to myself and God that I would stop stealing after my last arrest. I knew this time that I would be transported to jail.

Since a petty theft conviction with a prior petty theft conviction is a felony, I had fears of going to San Quentin State Prison.

This time a rookie police officer was sent so I didn't have to suffer the indignity of arrest like I did the first time that I was arrested. However, since I knew all of the jail workers, there would be enough embarrassment to go around.

The police officer completed his report, and then called the patrol wagon. I recognized both wagon men but they did not recognize me. It was a different story once at the jail.

There was a small inside parking area which led to a corridor which was attached to the rear door of the jail. Once an officer with a prisoner is identified outside, the door is opened from the inside and the prisoner is escorted into a secure room.

"Mike....Mike is that you?" said the voice on the PA system.

I immediately recognized the voice as Jeff. Jeff and I worked on the same squad years ago and he was currently the jail sergeant. I reluctantly answered, "Yeah. It's me."

"I don't believe it. Michael Givens. What happened to you? You were the best of the best when you were on the department."

I ignored the comment. Jeff obviously noticed my embarrassment because he ceased broadcasting on the PA system.

Before long, most of the jail's staff were coming into the prisoner search area to greet me. Some of them appeared happy to see me. Others just looked at me, shook their heads and walked away.

I was then placed in a holding cell and waited to be processed. There were nine or ten people in there with me in this cell that was built to house half that many.

I was fingerprinted and processed by Sgt. Haines. When Haines was a rookie, I trained him to be a police officer. Now he was fingerprinting his teacher. I think that he was more embarrassed than I was.

Because I was arrested on a Friday, I had to wait until Monday to be arraigned. I was transported to the county facility in Dublin, Ca. on Friday night.

The worst part of that experience was waiting in the bull pen with a group of other arrestees waiting to be processed. It was impossible to get comfortable on those cement benches when you are shoulder to shoulder with the next guy at Santa Rita Jail. I was in the bull pen for 13 hours before being led to a small room where I was given fashionable jail apparel, then led into a room with fifteen or twenty other men.

I remember thinking that this whole arrest and jail thing was inconvenient and interrupted my life. Not only did it interrupt my drug using, but it made it impossible for me to continue to destroy my life.

Once in the conference room, I was forced to bear the humiliation of a full body cavity search which included bending over, grabbing my butt cheeks and spreading them apart, and allowing another grown man to look up my ass.

After another 6 hours of this indignation, I was lead to my cell. I spent those two days sleeping; waking only for meals. My waking hours were spent praying and promising God that I would never use again.

The problem with that logic is that will power is almost never enough. I had lots of will power. For example: at the drop of a dime I <u>will</u> get high or I <u>will</u> steal. What I needed was <u>won't</u> power to prevent me from doing those things.

I thought that I could do it without God's help and I didn't bother asking Him for any.

The meals were horrible and the portions were small. I remember thinking that if the food taste bad, at least give me a lot of it. When I'm given just a little bit of terrible tasting food, I feel like I'm being cheated twice.

I was not worried about being recognized by other inmates as being an ex-police officer because so much time had passed since I was on the department.

On Monday morning, I was awakened at five in the morning and escorted to a bull pen along with other inmates in order to go to court. We arrived at the courthouse at about eight o'clock and were placed in a crowded bull pen where I had to wait until 4:30 PM before making a very brief appearance before the judge.

The public defender had already told me that I would not be charged with the felony if I plead guilty. He said that I would be charged with violation of my probation and given community service.

The judge and public defender proved to be in lockstep and I was told that when released that I should register with the community service office for assignment. I never did.

For some reason, I thought that I would be released and free to walk out of the courtroom. That is the way they do it on Matlock. I guess it's different in real life.

I was escorted, in chains to the bus and driven back to the Santa Rita Jail in Dublin and placed back in that damn bullpen, shoulder to shoulder and waited four hours before being brought back to my cell.

That was a long day. I had been awakened at five in the morning the escorted back to my cell at three o'clock the next morning in order to spend five minutes in front of the judge. I was not released until about two in the afternoon the next day.

EVERY ADDICT STOPS USING EVENTUALLY. SOME EVEN LIVE THROUGH IT!

I felt energized after those two days of sleep. So did my addict. The addict in me hit the ground running, skipping not one beat.

I went directly to my job at the Mexican nightclub, explained why I wasn't at work for the weekend and borrowed forty dollars from my boss. Then I wasted no time finding my way to the dope man.

A female that was known to me as Mary had a room at my favorite hotel. I spent the night in her room and we got high.

Mary had a visitor whose name was Dawn. I could tell just by looking at her that she was relatively new at smoking crack.

"Michael, why are you staring at me?" Dawn said.

"I'm sorry Dawn. I did not mean to stare. I was just thinking and I hope you don't mind my asking but how long have you been smoking this shit?"

"About four months."

"I see. I hope you don't mind my telling you that you have made the biggest mistake of your life. You may not realize it now because you are in what's called the honeymoon period of your addiction. Right now you are enjoying the high you get when you take a hit and you are probably thinking that you are choosing to get loaded, but you are not. The honeymoon will last up to a year. Then it goes from being pleasurable to being a burden. A burden that you will carry with you 24-7. The fun is over and you are hooked. The silly part about the whole ordeal is that your brain thinks that you are still having fun. That's the insanity. My advice to you would be to do anything but smoke this shit. Drink heavily or pop pills. Anything but this shit. It's may be too late for me. You see. I've been smoking this shit for many years. I lost the woman that I love, my family, houses, cars and everything and everyone that I hold dear because I chose to smoke this shit. I've even lost myself several times. It's not too late for you."

My advice seem to go in one ear and out the other. After all; she was on her honeymoon.

The next morning Mary asked if I wanted to be her semi-permanent room mate. She proposed that we both pay half of the rent which was due at eleven o'clock each day.

I agreed but I told her that I would not have the rent until five o'clock. Mary said that she would cover the rent for that day. She then got out of bed, got dressed, left the room at 9AM, turned a trick and was back at 10:15AM with the rent money and crack to smoke.

I was one day out of jail and back to my old thieving ways. I recognized the fact that there was only a matter of time before I was caught again. I was running in and out of stores two or three times a day. Sooner or later the law of averages will catch up with me and I would be back in the County detention facility.

I heard that the Oakland Coliseum was hiring concession workers. I applied and was hired. It was the perfect part time job. I selected what sporting events I wanted to work and the pay was good. I decided to work the games that did not conflict with the nights I worked at the Mexican nightclub.

I was lucky enough to be selected to work at a beer booth. Fans that purchased beer were big tippers. It was not unusual for me to make more that one hundred dollars in six hours in tips alone.

This was the perfect job for a dope fiend. I was able to keep my agreement with Mary and feed my addiction at the same time.

When Mary went to jail for three weeks for solicitation, I was able to keep the room until she was released.

During baseball season, I worked three or four days per week on most weeks. Things changed when the A's baseball season ended. The Raiders played at home once every two weeks so I had to revert to stealing to again to supplement my income.

I devised a scheme that involved lil trees automobile air fresheners. I would walk into a store and take all the trees of the shelves. I would them sell them at a strip mall in east Oakland: three for one dollar.

One Friday, I entered a particular drug store and snaked through the aisles to make sure that I was not followed. I then found my way to the automotive aisle where I removed every lil tree from the shelves and stuffed them down my pants and inside my jacket. I felt that someone was watching me, but I cared not. My addict needed those trees.

Hesitating not, I walked out of the front door. I turned and saw two plain clothes guards running in my direction. Like a jet, I took off across the parking lot, throwing trees into the air. When they caught me I had not one tree on me and customers were in the parking lot picking them up like candy.

As I sat hand-cuffed in the rear of the store, I remember asking myself over and over, "Mike, what the hell are you doing." It's amazing how clearly you can see things when life gives you pause. When you can do nothing but sit there and think of the error of your ways. But it was too late to feel sorry for myself.

I had this sick sunken feeling in my gut as I thought that the judge would surely send me to San Quentin this time. I lucked out last time that he did not charge me with the theft. He merely violated my probation. I knew that I would not be so lucky this time.

I was transported to the Oakland jail in the patrol wagon. On the way I continuously prayed that God would give me a way out of this situation.

I was so thin my clothes felt like they were going to fall off of me. A jailer told me that I looked like death, sitting on a tombstone, eating lifesavers.

I told the nurse that I had a headache. When she took my blood pressure, she told the jail sergeant that she would not allow me in the jail. The nurse said that my blood pressure was at stroke level and that I would have to go to the hospital first.

That meant that an officer would have to stand watch over me. Since the police department was short handed, I was given a citation, driven to the Alameda County hospital and released in the parking lot. Staff in the emergency room gave me medication for my hypertension then I went to my room.

I felt that I had dodged a bullet. Then I thought about the prayers that I sent up the brief time that I was in custody and I thanked God for his mercy and grace.

I thought of the many times that I put myself in situations that I thought were inescapable and God made a means of escape. I felt that I was not worthy of his grace and protection. There had been so many times that I had made promises to him and then broken those promises.

This time was no different. My behavior changed not and neither did the consequences.

After a couple of months of living in hopelessness, I was a passenger in a car that was stopped by the police in San Leandro, Ca. The police officer ran my name for warrants and found that I had one for one hundred fifty dollars for not showing up for court on my first petty theft arrest and another one for five hundred dollars for not showing up for community service.

San Leandro jail was heaven compared to Oakland. There was a small town jailhouse feel to it. I was expecting Barney Fife to walk in any minute.

But this heaven did not last. I was transported to the county jail in Dublin where I spent hour upon hour in the bullpen before being dressed and strip searched and shown to my cell.

Up at five in the morning and court by eight, I waited all day for my brief court appearance. Judge Moyers sentenced me to six weeks in jail. Suddenly I was not in a rush to get back to my cell.

The next few weeks were the longest weeks in life. Not withstanding my claustrophobia, jail is the worst place in the world for an addict. All options are taken away and you lose control of your life and freedom. You can do nothing without permission so you sleep all day locked away in a small cell.

After my second day I was climbing the walls. We were let out of our cells only for meals, and since the facility was on lockdown during the time I was there, there was no TV time.

There is a lot of time for thinking during incarceration. I thought about my family much of the time. I was in the habit of disappearing any time I started using. I did not want my family to see the things that I was capable of doing or how bad I looked.

When my son was a boy, he was so proud of his dad. He would brag to his friends about having a dad that was a police officer.

So when I started using, I just disappeared. Poof. Vanished in mid air. I knew that my disappearance was rooted in shame, embarrassment and disgrace, but I was powerless to do anything about it.

In the end, I realize those emotions I felt were self centered. My family cared more about the fact that I was OK. They worried when I was missing. They knew not whether I was dead or alive so they worried even more.

My mother had the prayer warriors at the Market Street Church in Oakland praying for me and I am convinced that I am alive and in my right mind as a result of their prayers.

During my brief stay at the Santa Rita jail, I relived everyday of my addiction. Every hit, from my first hit to my latest. I tried to recall the last time I actually enjoyed the experience. I drew a blank.

Most of my time getting high was spent in turmoil and confusion. It had become a burden.I surrounded myself with murderers and robbers and their behavior had rubbed off on me.

I heard it said once that if you hang out in a barber shop long enough, sooner or later you'll get a haircut.

I spoke differently. I walked differently. I looked different. I thought differently.

Every hit I took, I lost a little bit of myself. There were no good times worth reminiscing about. In fact most of the good times in the last few years were spent while I was in recovery.

It was about four in the afternoon when I was awakened by the loud sound of fist against my cell door.

"Michael Givens, get your stuff together you are going home."

That was music to my ears. I had no idea what day of the week it was or how much time I had spent in that hell hole and I did not care. I had stopped keeping track of time weeks prior. This experience served to convince me that jail isn't the place to be. It ain't fun.

I was confused as to the direction that my life would take. Though I recalled all of those bad experiences of smoking crack, I was dumbfounded by the fact that I wasn't ready to quit yet, and I had no idea why.

I was released by seven o'clock and I took a train directly to my and Mary's room. When I got to the room, I thought it strange that the lights were off in the room but the inside latch lock was engaged.

I knocked and heard Mary's voice...

"Who is it?"

"It's me. Open the door."

She was very excited to see me and appeared afraid. She threw her arms around my neck and would not release.

"What is wrong with you?" I asked.

For some unknown reason, Mary had always called me Gunner.

"Gunner you don't know what's been going on around here. There's a gang of guys in the neighborhood going around robbing people. Two of them just got out of prison and they are robbing and beating people on the street, taking money from whores and their tricks and kicking in hotel room doors. That's why I had the lights off."

"Well I hope they don't try to rob us tonight. I am not in the mood and I will shoot anyone that comes through that door without proper authorization. Where is my gun anyway?"

"I've been sleeping with it under my pillow."

"Well do me a favor and put it under my pillow. Let's leave this hell hole of a hotel tomorrow and get a room across town. The rent is the same and the area is a little better for you to hustle."

The next day, we did not move from the room as planned, but I took extra precautions when in the neighborhood. I went nowhere without my gun.

But all the precautions in the world wouldn't have prepared me for what happened the following week.

I had just received my pay from the Mexican nightclub when I walked into the room. I gave Mary twenty five dollars and told her go purchase some dope. While she was gone and as a precaution, I put all but eighteen dollars in the garbage can, between the plastic bag and the can. I then went into the bathroom.

While in there I heard Mary come in the door. When I opened the bathroom door, I saw Mary and three men I had never seen before. Each of the three men had a gun. One of them had two guns. I recognized one of the guns as being mine.

"Whoa...wasup?"I said

"Nigga... you know wasup. You know what this is. Break yourself."

One of them grabbed me and pushed me against a wall and searched me, He took the eighteen dollars bait money I had in my pocket and told me to lay on the floor next to Mary. I later learned that they had taken the crack that Mary had bought for me. From the vantage point of laying face down on the floor, I could see the garbage can that I put the rest of my money.

They ransacked the room looking for more money but found it not. One of them even picked up the garbage can and went through it, but he didn't remove the plastic lining which would have revealed the $320 I put there.

When they finally left, I told Mary to pack her things. I called a cab and I have not been back to that hotel since.

The police pulled the cab over as it pulled away from the hotel. The officers said that someone called in a disturbance in our room. The officer ran us for warrants. Mary had a felony warrant and was escorted to jail. Mary was gone for eighteen months.

I really felt the prayer warriors that time. That group of robbers had a reputation of beating their victims, yet they barely laid hands on . This was just one of many times that I have dodged the bullet. God was working overtime watching over me.

The insanity that had become my life was growing daily.

INSANITY- DOING THE SAME THINGS, BUT EXPECTING DIFFERENT RESULTS.

Alcoholics anonomous

I don't recall what result I was expecting. I continued doing the same things and was arrested on another petty theft charge. I went through the same set of emotions that I felt every time I was arrested. Shame, guilt, disgust, embarrassment and humiliation.

I was sure that I was San Quentin bound this time. I thought that my luck had run out for sure this time.

Again, I was arrested on a Friday. I appeared in court on Monday and noticed that I had caught the same judge as last time. Judge Moyers took his time reviewing each of my previous arrests before asking for my plea.

"Mr. Givens, I see that you have found yourself back in my court again. Apparently you have not learned your lesson after previous appearances. Mr. Givens I'm going to give you one more chance at changing your ways. I'm going to violate your probation for the last time. If I see you in my court or if you appear in any other court, I will make sure that you are put so far under San Quentin that they will have to pump sunshine to you. Do you understand? I'm sentencing you to time served and three years probation."

"Yes you honor. I understand."

I really did understand the judge. I did not want to go to prison and was ready to do what was necessary to remain a free man. My life of thievery was over. I have not stolen as much as a grape since.

But the addict still needed to thrive.

I needed another hustle. I needed a legal hustle because my addict had not the patience to go out and get a job .

The day after I was released, I asked a recycler to show me how he made his living.

I grabbed a shopping cart and started my recycling business.

There is an art to recycling bottles and cans. The secret is to discover what days the neighborhoods have trash pick up, and when the trash is put out remove the bottles and cans from the recycle bins. If done right, it's relatively easy to make more than one hundred dollars per day.

At first it was difficult because other recyclers were hesitant to tell me what areas were collected on a given day, so it was trial and error until I figured out the garbage pick up routes for the city on my own.

Maria, the owner of the Mexican night club was extremely understanding concerning my occasional jail stays and reserved my job for me every time I went. So between my job and buggy recycling, I found it easy to pay the $45.00 per day motel rent. The rest of my money was spent on food and crack.

I had become friendly with a drug dealer whose name was Slick. After a few months I started grinding, which meant that I sold small amounts of crack that I bought from Slick at a discount and then I smoked up the profits, saving just enough to buy an amount to sell in order to keep the cycle going.

I became popular with local panhandlers and small time hustlers. I sat in the same spot everyday and sold and smoked crack. At times I gave away more of the drug than I smoked to "friends".

I stayed awake for days at a time and did this for months until I noticed that my health was beginning to deteriorate. I had not taken any blood pressure medicine for months and I could walk for no more than a block without resting. My ankles were swollen and I was constantly out of breath.

I was sitting at "the spot" one day when I starting having chest pains. I asked several of "my friends" to walk to the phone booth which was a block away to call 911 because I felt that I was having a heart attack. All of "my friends" refused to go.

I reminded them of the drugs I had given them for free. Still no one would stop hitting their pipes long enough to go. Holding my chest, I got up while in great pain and walked to the phone booth by myself.

The paramedics arrived and told me that I was in the process of having a heart attack and that my blood pressure was through the roof. I was then they rushed to Highland hospital.

Once at Highland, I was given medicine that in time lowered my blood pressure. Doctors told me that because of my uncontrolled blood pressure and drug use I had an enlarged heart and congestive heart failure.

I was told that I needed to take my medication regularly and to stay off my feet for a few days. I was released from the hospital after six days.

I went directly to slick's house because he owed me money. I then returned to "the spot "and witnessed "my friends" sitting there tweaking. Because they had no money or drugs they seemed genuinely interested in my well being.

I told them to go and screw themselves (and I did not use the word screw).

I recycled by night and grinded by day and took my blood pressure medicine on a regular basis for a while.

By choice, I was alone most of the time. There are no such things as friends when you are on the street.

FOR EVERY SMILE I RECEIVED ON THE STREET THERE'S A MATCHING KNIFE WOUND IN MY BACK.

Every one wants something from you. If you don't have anything they want, they won't speak to you most of the time. Their goal is to get you into as much shit as possible.

I am reminded of the story of the not so smart bird that refused to fly south for the winter. He had decided that he loved the northern territory and wanted to make it his home.

Well, he was flying around one day and it became very cold. In fact it was so cold that his wings froze and the bird fell to the ground. The bird remained frozen on the ground until a bear came along and took a shit right on top of the him.

The warmth from this new environment thawed the little birds wings. It felt so good to the bird that the he started to sing.

A fox heard the bird singing, dug him out of the shit and ate him.

The moral of this story is: Everyone that gets you into shit isn't always your enemy. Everyone that gets you out of shit isn't always your friend. And if you are in a bunch of shit but you are comfortable and warm, shut the hell up!

Everyone has a game that they want to run or a trick that they want you to become entangled in. Nothing about the streets is caring and warm. Being caring and warm most of the time will get you hurt or killed in what's called the game.

THE GAME ISN'T A GAME AT ALL. IT'S A DEADLY SERIOUS, MORALLY DEPRIVED SERIES OF ACTIONS, DRIVEN BY SELF SERVING CHARACTERS WHOSE ONLY DESIGN IS TO SYSTEMATICALLY RELIEVE YOU OF EVERYTHING YOU HAVE.

Everyone <u>seems</u> trustworthy, but no-one can be trusted. Whenever someone is talking you can bet that what they are saying is a lie.

It is further complicated by the fact that no-one wants to be disrespected. The standard of disrespect is unique to each person. One man may feel disrespected if someone flirts with his girl. Another man may feel disrespected if someone looks at him the wrong way.

A drug dealer may feel disrespected if a drug user doesn't pay a debt.

Such was the case one day as I sat at the spot. A dope fiend whose name was Leroy walked in acting very friendly with everyone. That was a sign that he was broke. If he had dope or money he would've spoken to anyone or even establish eye contact.

Leroy sat at the small table directly across from me. There were seven other people there. I grew tired of Leroy's constant rambling so I went into the bathroom to finish the small amount of drugs that I had. I was in the bathroom for less than ten minutes when I heard two gun shots. I waited a minute or two before I came out of the bathroom. I walked into the living room to find everyone gone except Leroy, who was on the floor with two gunshot wounds to his head. I immediately left the spot.

I later learned that Leroy was executed by a drug dealer whom he owed twenty dollars to. The problem was not the twenty dollars, but the disrespect caused by Leroy by not paying.

Why would anyone <u>decide</u> to live this way?

That day, I realized how tenuous life is. I had elected to mingle with madmen and in the process placed my own life in limbo.

I had decided to abandon the loving company of family and friends in order to completely surround myself with street demons and sexual deviants and I feared that I was becoming one of them.

Even the way I spoke was negatively affected by my associations. My sentences were filled with profanity and hyperbole.

I was lost in a wasteland of selfishness, greed and loneliness. What happened to Leroy that day could have easily happened to me on a different day. What happened to Leroy that day changed my thinking.

After living the street life for years, this moment of clarity prompted me to call Palm Avenue detox in San Mateo County. I had remembered hearing of Palm Avenue from a sober addict months prior.

He told me that it is a good place to rest for a week and get that shit out of my system. He also told me that the food was good, the staff was caring and that it was free.

The price was certainly right so I called as soon as I got to my room after the shooting. I told the person on the phone that I was a dope fiend that needed help. The soft spoken person on the phone told me that there were no beds available and I needed to call at 11AM everyday until a bed became available.

I called everyday and after the fourth day a bed became available. I was told that I would need to get there on my own which was a task because of the distance, lack of money and the fact that they would only save the bed until 3 PM.

I purchased the minimum priced BART train ticket with my last money and prayed that there would be a kind station agent at the Millbrae Station who would grant me passage without the added fee.

When I arrived in Millbrae, I explained my quandary and this angel of a station agent not only allowed me through the gate without the added fee, but also gave me the two dollars I needed for bus fare to complete my journey.

I arrived at Palm Avenue at about 2:45 PM.

The detox is located in an unassuming building in the middle of a non-descript block. I walked into the small office and was greeted by a smiling gentleman that introduced himself as Jeff.

Jeff completed my intake then led me through the elongated dining and kitchen area and through the rear door where most of the residents were out smoking cigarettes. After introducing me to them Jeff showed me to my bed.

The sleeping quarters were a series of rooms aligned on the same side of the dining room. There were four beds in each of the six large rooms.

In the kitchen there were two huge refrigerators stocked with food and juice that was available to residents 24 hours a day. There was also a table that was loaded with snacks such as sandwich foods, cookies, crackers and cakes.

After the tour I took a shower then attacked the refrigerators like a savage. I drank at least a gallon of apple and cranberry juice. Being on the street getting high, it's easy to forget to eat.

After this mammoth of a feast, I got into my bed and slept the remainder of the night. I was lucky to have found this place.

During intake I was asked where I would like to go after my seventh day. I told Jeff that I wished to be placed in a sober living environment but not particularly a program because I wanted to work a job while working on myself. I thought that starting a new life in San Mateo County would be good for my recovery since I knew no-one and drugs were not in my face all the time like they were in Oakland.

Jeff told me about a place in Redwood City, CA. that would fit my needs. The place is called Maple Street. Jeff placed me on the waiting list.

The purpose of the detox is to give the addict a place to rest while the immediate affects of the drug wear off. Also to give the addict food so that he can begin to re-establish his health.

There were also AA meetings on the property. I took full advantage of every opportunity offered. The food was excellent and the employees were accommodating.

Palm Ave was a God send. I felt rejuvenated and ready to take on the world at the end of the seven days.

Once there was a bed at Maple St., the staff informed me, but I was already ready to go.

After a short intake at Maple St., I was granted a tour. I was first shown my bunk. I was given a top bunk in a large room that had at least 20 sets of bunks.

There were two large TV rooms at the facility, each with a big screen TV and lots of movies.

The staff member told me that after thirty days I would be given an opportunity to move to the transitional side of the same building. There, I would be given my own small room, extended curfew hours and other benefits.

There were counselors on the property that encouraged residents to find jobs and we were required to participate in the money management program. Each payday we were required to save at least sixty percent of our take home pay in order to procure an apartment at a later date.

Within two weeks I had secured employment with Kinkos. I worked there for about two months before I was offered a temp to perm job with an employment agency working in a call center as a customer service agent. That job became permanent after three months and I had saved a substantial amount of money in my money management account.

I used some of the money I had saved to buy a car that had been donated to Saint Vincent DePaul.

I was a frequent attendee at AA and NA meetings in San Mateo County. I thought that my recovery was going well.

I had six months clean and I thought that I was cured so I stop going to meetings. I thought that I could wing it so I never tried to work the steps.

I thought that after I stop using for a while, that I could go back to living the life I lived before I started using. I was wrong.

That person died when I took that first hit too many years ago. If I am to move forward I will have to become a whole new person and start doing things like I've never done them before. I will eventually have to reinvent myself.

I NEVER WANT TO BE THE PERSON I WAS BEFORE I STARTED USING BECAUSE THE PERSON I WAS BEFORE I STARTED USING, STARTED USING.

My addict was also working against me. Without clueing me in to what he was thinking, my addict was planning and plotting ways to undermine my sobriety. I should have recognized the signs, though they were subtle.

His rise to dominance begins in ways that are barely noticeable at first. My addict did things like force me to remember the "good times" that I had getting loaded and ignoring the disasters. He encouraged me to drive through the old neighborhood for no good reason. He suggested that I should stop doing the things that I did to get sober in the first place.

I gave the addict power by "glorifying" the drug when involved in conversation with sober friends.

I have a disease that is triggered by my own thinking. Just as a person trying to avoid the flu distances himself from people that cough and sneeze, an addict has to distance himself from poisonous thoughts. Just as a person tries to avoid HIV by not participating in unsafe sex, an addict must at all cost avoid unsafe thinking.

We control our thoughts only with practice, patience and discipline. Much work is required and there is no standing still.

YOU ARE EITHER BUSY WORKING ON YOU RECOVERY OR YOU ARE BUSY WORKING ON YOUR RELAPSE.

Well I stopped working on my recovery and soon I was on another run.

My addict had convinced me that I needed to drive to Oakland and didn't bother to give me a reason why. "It is just a nice day to drive to Oakland" he said, and I said "OK."

Once there, I ran into a female dope fiend that had always wanted to get with me but I never gave her the opportunity to. Before I knew it, she was in my car and we were on our way to buy some crack. I rented a room and we got high all day and evening. After the dope was gone, of course, there was the dissatisfaction and irritability that running out of the drug can bring.

I missed curfew a Maple St. and failed the drug test the next day. I was asked by staff to leave immediately.

I took this relapse particularly hard. For the first time in my addiction, my self doubt ran deep. I questioned my ability to stay clean.

I was particular hard on myself because of issues involving my son whom I hadn't seen in several years. I was raised by a loving mother in a fatherless household and I never wanted to pass that legacy on to Mike Jr.

I thought that he would never know how much I love him or how sorry I am that I missed so many years of his development. I can offer no excuses. I must accept full responsibility for my inaction on his behalf. I can only pray that God will have as much mercy on him as he has had on me.

In the past, I had always believed that one day there would be "the last hit" and that I would walk away and never turn back. Suddenly, I was unsure that day would ever come. I felt that I had no say so in my own life anymore. That my life was controlled by forces that I no longer could defeat.

I had unwittingly worked the first step.

WE ADMITTED THAT WE WERE POWERLESS OVER OUR ADDICTION AND THAT OUR LIVES HAD BECOME UNMANAGEABLE.

Even though I felt my lack of control, I was not ready to admit it. I hadn't recognized that milestone in my recovery until several years later because I had allowed my addict to regain control of my life again.

Maple St. had given me the money that I contributed to my money management account. I rented a room at a residential hotel in Oakland and did not resurface for a week. I didn't even bother to call my job.

I did little but get high for the next month or so. I was nearly broke when, out of desperation, I called my old friend Ralph. He was concerned because he had not heard from me in such a long time. He told me to meet him at a meeting and I did so.

After the meeting we had coffee at Starbucks.

"Ralph my friend, let me tell you what I've been through…"

"There is no need for you to do that. I already know. You forget that I am an addict too. You have gone through the same thing most addicts have to go through. Your story is no different. It is full of the incomprehensible insanity that can get you killed. I told you once that recovery is not an event. It is a process. A process that will continue until one day you finally get it or until you die. Very few addicts stop using on the first try. That's just the way it is for most of us. We have to hit rock bottom. Then we have to hit rock bottom again. Each time rock bottom gets deeper and deeper. Then one day you get it. So don't be too hard on yourself. You are not bad, getting good. You are sick, getting better. And every time you put yourself through what you are putting yourself through, you get a little bit better.

EVERY ADDICT STOPS USING EVENTUALLY. SOME OF THEM EVEN LIVE THROUGH IT."

My friend Ralph is a very wise man. I left our little meeting feeling a little better about my situation.

I wondered what it will take for me to finally "get it". How long will I have to wander in this desert before finding my way out? Every time I see what I think is the end of this hopeless journey in this desert, what I see turns out to be a mirage. So the journey continues.

Maybe the problem was the fact that I was wandering with out direction. I was strong and eager to go, but I knew not what direction to go so I just roamed the desert hopelessly.

HOPE IS THAT THING THAT GIVES STRENGTH DIRECTION

Maybe that's it. I possessed all the strength that I needed. What I needed was to regain the hope I once had in order to see past the mirage.

My wanderings lead me to the Will Rogers Hotel. The Will Rogers was a run down, roach, rat and dope fiend infested, hell hole of a Hotel in downtown Oakland that rented rooms for $90 per week. This place was a joke.

There was a crack smoker in every room and on the first of each month, when welfare and social security checks were dispensed; there was so much crack smoke in the air in the halls I found it difficult to navigate my way to my room without bumping into a wall or two. And I'm not even exaggerating much.

There were legions of scantily clad prostitutes that randomly knocked on room doors in the middle of the night in search of tricks and crack.

I had convinced Maria to give me my job back at the Mexican nightclub, but I only worked two days per week. The pay I received at the nightclub was adequate to pay my rent. I recycled bottles and cans to earn money for food and crack.

I had lived at the Will Rogers for four months and my rent for the week was past due. Management had told me that when I returned from work this day that my possessions would be on the sidewalk outside.

But when I arrived, instead I saw smoke and flames coming from a fourth floor window of the hotel. The residents were standing outside admiring the flames.

One of them told me that someone on the fourth floor was smoking crack and caused the fire. That person died in the fire.

The Red Cross was there with buses. The residents were told to board the buses and we were taken to a local high school. We were given cots and a meal and we slept there in the gym that night.

The next morning the Red Cross buses took us to the Holiday Inn and paid for us to stay there for two weeks. 150 dope fiends at the nice and clean Holiday Inn for two weeks. That hotel will never be the same.

I signed on to a lawsuit filed by residents of the Will Rogers for conditions that existed at the hotel before the fire. I never thought that we would ever see a penny.

When the two weeks at the Holiday Inn were up, the Red Cross also paid for us to stay at a residential hotel for a week. I knew that the Red Cross did good work, but I never thought that they would do so much for a bunch of hopeless dope fiends.

I went to the Red Cross office and explained to them that I had nowhere to go after the stay at the residential hotel. I told them that I was working but didn't have the deposit and first month rent for an apartment..

The Red Cross decided to pay my deposit and first month rent when I found an apartment. I signed an agreement to rent an apartment at the California Hotel Apartments in west Oakland.

I remain eternally grateful to the Red Cross of Northern California for their caring and action.

I lived at the California for three months and never once bothered to pay rent. My addiction to crack cocaine continued to make a fool out of me. I was evicted after the third month.

Again, I was homeless and on the street. After several months, I called Palm Ave and was told to keep calling until there was a bed. This time it only took two days for them to find a bed for me. Ralph gave me a ride to San Mateo County this time. I requested and received a bed at Maple Street after a seven day stint at Palm Ave.

I kept what Ralph had told me in mind while in detox and I was determined to make it this time.

I had gotten a job as a stock clerk at a local supermarket and was rebuilding my money management account when I received a letter from the lawyer handling the Will Rogers lawsuit.

The letter stated that I should report to the lawyer's office and that the suit had been settled. My share was six thousand dollars and change. I could not believe my eyes. I had forgotten about the law suit months prior.

IF YOU THINK THAT YOU CAN OR IF YOU THINK THAT YOU CAN'T, YOU ARE PROBABLY RIGHT.

I know not if the check put me in relapse mode or if I was in relapse mode before I opened the envelope, but when I saw the numbers on the check, it felt as if I had just taken a hit. My mouth became dry and my head started spinning.

I knew that I had to spend the lion's share of the money immediately or I would kill myself so I sold my old car and bought a late model Suburban. I got an excellent deal on the truck and it looked and operated like new. I also gave some of the money to my mother.

Each time I relapsed it became more and more difficult for me to get high. I have attributed it to the fact that I was becoming a stronger person. Though I was still operating on self will and remain unable to defeat the beast that lurked within me, I was becoming strong enough to admit that I was powerless.

I HAD GAINED ENOUGH POWER TO ADMIT THAT I HAD NO POWER.

I had remembered what my friend Ralph had said to me. Recovery is not an event. It is a process. I am not bad, getting good. I am sick, getting better.

Within weeks, I had left Maple Street and paid two weeks rent for a room in Oakland. I had returned to the life I had given up so many times before.

I locked myself in my room and only left occasionally to eat or to buy more dope. I had lost fifteen pounds in two weeks and I had stopped taking my blood pressure medicine.

Within weeks I was nearly broke. I sold my Suburban to an auto wholesaler for one thousand dollars less than I had paid for it.

I paid rent for a month then locked myself in my room. I had lost so much weight that none of my clothes would fit me properly. My face was sucked up to the point that it looked like a skeleton with skin on it. I paid little attention to my personal hygiene and I showered seldomly.

The rental period and my money ran out at about the same time which meant that I was on the street with no money.

I learned of a spot under the freeway at Sycamore St. and Northgate St. in Oakland that other homeless had made a camp. I went there and "reserved "a spot. The next day I found a futon and mattress and carried it to my new home.

Recycling became my means of income again. This time I really looked the part. My clothes were dirty and my personal hygiene was absent.

There are different ways to gauge your appearance on the street. If I were to walk up to a drug dealer that I did not know on the street and he flat out refused to sell me dope and ask if I were a cop, I would know that I didn't look bad at all. If, on the other hand, the stranger looks me up and down before reluctantly selling me the drug, I would know that I was on my way down. But if the unknown dealer were to see me walking in his direction from a block away and he yells, "Hey, I got it right here" I'd know that I'm one sucked up dope fiend.

My shopping cart became my constant companion. I went nowhere without it and it seemed like that all I did was work and smoke. It was difficult, but I managed to maintain a sense of dignity.

I was pushing my buggy at Telegraph Ave. and Grand Ave. in Oakland where I saw a man laying in the middle of Telegraph Ave. not moving. At first I thought that he had been the victim of a vehicle collision but when I approached I realized that he was snot slinging drunk.

I helped the well dressed older brother to his feet and sat him at the bus stop. There was also a homeless man sleeping at the bus stop. The drunken fellow told me that his ride would arrive in twenty minutes so I waited with him.

Out of gratitude, my inebriated friend removed a huge wad of money from his pocket. There were several one hundred dollar bills among the twenties and smaller bills.

He peeled off a one dollar bill and gave it to me out of appreciation for my helping hin. He fumbled with the money and dropped half of the wad on the ground. All of this activity caught the attention of the now awake homeless guy.

I got the impression that the homeless man wanted to rob the drunkard, so I stayed with him until his ride arrived.

I helped the gentleman into the waiting vehicle and he was gone.

When I got back to the camp, I told my fellow dope fiends of my adventures and was roundly criticized for not robbing the helpless alcoholic. They argued that he would not have remembered what I looked like because he was so drunk.

I explained to them that I did not think that taking his money was the right thing to do. I also told them that God rewards good deeds. I told them that something good would happen to me within two days.

None of them believed me or understood why I did not take that guy's money.

The very next day I was recycling in the same area. Construction crews were building an office building on Grand Ave just east of Telegraph. I approached the job's foreman and asked about recycling at the job cite.

The conversation eventually turned to religion and church. The foreman told me that he taught Sunday school at his church and that he occasionally gave sermons.

I told him of my church and that I had not attended lately because of my sinful way of life.

I don't remember his name, but this kind gentleman that I had never seen before in life looked at me and said, "You know, I feel that God wants me to do something special for you."

He then reached into his wallet, removed a bill and placed it in my hand. I did not look at the bill. I just said, "Thank you" and walked away. I was halfway down the block when I looked and noticed that I had a one hundred dollar bill in my hand. I turned around but the foreman was gone.

I made it back to the camp and told a few people what had happened. They didn't believe me and accused me of taking the money from the drunkard.

I did not care what they thought. I know that God sends angels at times when we are at need. That includes to us sinners.

Three days later, I was walking in front of an office building when I noticed what looked like a cell phone laying on the ground. I picked it up and discovered that it was a Blackberry that was still active.

I tried to contact the owner by calling some of the contacts listed in the phones memory but I could contact no one.

I was about six blocks away from where I had found the device when it began to ring. I answered. It was the phone's owner. He was very happy that I had found the phone and said that his whole life was on that phone.

I turned and walked back to the building and met the owner in front. We talked for a few minutes and when I was about to leave he said, "Wait a minute" then handed me five twenty dollar bills. I thanked him and walked away.

I am convinced that if I had taken the drunkard's money, I would never have met the foreman nor the Blackberry owner and that a series of bad things would have occurred in my life.

Some call it karma. I choose to give the credit to God.

I think that at times, we make it hard for God to bless us. We leave no room for him to operate. We shut him out by trying to bless ourselves at every opportunity by taking advantage of others or by doing illegal things.

The foreman had told me about a program in Berkeley for alcoholic and drug addicts. He said that the program is called Options and that it was comprehensive.

I called Options and the voice on the phone instructed me to come in the following day.

Options had a relationship with a shelter. I lived there for thirty days before moving into transitional housing owned by Options.

The program was conducted on an out patient basis and included structured classes, groups and meetings. Acupuncture, Yoga and Tai Chi were mandatory activities offered by the program. A typical day started at 8 AM and ended at 2 PM.

Transitional housing was certainly better than living under the freeway. I had lived under the freeway for over six months and had forgotton what it was like to take a shower anytime I wanted to or to go to the refrigerator and get something to eat when I was hungry.

Options is very well structured. Too bad that I wasn't serious about recovering this time. I needed a rest and a chance to reorganize after being outside for so long.

While still in the program, I bought a small truck. Three days after making the purchase, I left the program.

I regret the fact that I left Options without paying rent for transitional housing. The people there were very good to me. I will repay them one day.

It was much easier to make money with a truck. I recycled everything from bottles and cans to cardboard, wooden pallets and metal. The money was good enough for me to rent a motel room everyday.

It would have been cheaper for me to rent an apartment rather than spend the forty five dollars per day I paid for my room, but an apartment required advance planning and saving money and there was no room in my life for that. I had very few priorities that didn't involve crack cocaine.

I would work all day and then lock myself in my room and get loaded all night. I lived a very lonely and quiet existence for over a year. I preferred being alone. I was free of the drama that being with others could bring.

The fact that I made more money translated into the fact that I smoked more drugs. In fact, my drug smoking was at an all time high. I did little else.

Eventually my truck, mostly because of differed maintenance issues, stopped running and was towed by the city.

I was forced to resort back to my buggy thus limiting my income. I was no longer able to recycle metal, cardboard and pallets. I was still able to make rent everyday but it seemed like all I did was work.

EVERY SET-BACK IS A SET-UP FOR A COMEBACK!

10

I GET IT

I was caught in a trap, I saw no way out and I was tired of trying. Physically, I was exhausted. Mentally, I was drained, emotionally, I was a wreck, and psychologically, I thought that I had lost my mind. I had not taken my blood pressure medicine in months.

This crack thing had gotten the best of me. I did not think that I had the strength in my body to live a sober life. I no longer felt that there would be a day that I would feel that I could live without the drug. In fact I no longer had a desire to live.

I had decided to end my life by overdosing on crack.

I purchased a quarter ounce of crack and sat alone in my dark room. I placed the baggie containing the drug on the little round table near the door and I had a conversation with it.

"Crack, you've won. I no longer have the strength or will to fight you anymore. For years, you have tried to destroy my life. You have taken everyone and everything away from me. I hope that you are happy now that you will have what you want. I just want you to know that I hate you and everything that you represent. You have taken from me everything worth having. Now; tonight, you will take my life."

I then removed a huge chunk of the drug placed it on my pipe. This was by far the most I had ever put into my body at one time. I prayed to God for forgiveness, and then I hit the pipe.

I did not expect to survive the dose, but I did. I then placed an even bigger piece of the poisonous drug on the pipe and hit that too. Still nothing. I continued this process until all of the drug was gone. I received nothing but a headache and chest pains for my troubles. I felt my pulse in my ears and my head throbbed incessantly.

I laid on my bed and cried. "I am even powerless to kill myself" I thought. I felt completely and utterly powerless.

Suddenly I felt a warm feeling run through my body. Though I was alone in this room I didn't feel lonely anymore. It was as if God himself had placed his hand on me and told me that he was in control.

I fervently prayed that he would remove this heavy burden from my shoulders because I was not strong enough to do so. I told him that I was entirely willing to turn my will and life over to him and whatever he wanted for life, I was willing to give. The warm soothing feeling persisted and I slept through the night.

The very next day I found myself on Piedmont Ave. in Oakland walking hard cement, pushing a heavy buggy diligently collecting bottles and cans. It was a cool and rainy night.

It was about four o'clock in the morning and I had been working this day since about 6 PM.

I would love to elaborate on the details of this night, but I can't, because I remember it not.

"Mr. Givens... Mr. Givens. Everything is alright. You have had open heart surgery. You can't talk because there is a breathing tube in your throat. Please try to relax", was the first thing I remember hearing as I awakened in a foggy haze in this strange environment. As my vision cleared, I noticed the smiling young nurse speaking with a heavy West African accent standing over me as I laid on a hospital bed in the intensive care ward at Summit Hospital.

"The doctor will come by later to remove your breathing tube. You are a very lucky man. Most people that undergo the type of surgery you underwent don't survive. You have visitors here to see you."

I turned my head as much as I could toward the door to see my mother enter the room. I later learned that she had maintained a constant vigil at my bedside during the three weeks that I was in a coma.

She was flanked by my older brother, Larry, who had taken leave from his job and flew here to Oakland California from his home in Canada out of concern for my well being. My younger brother Matthew and my gorgeous younger sister Lamarah were also present.

I was touched by their outpouring of love and affection.

Because of the combination of my not taking my hypertension medication and my addiction to crack and the failed suicide attempt of the night before, my tired heart had become bruised and battered from being overworked.

As a result, hematomas; not unlike the ones that pop up on your forehead when you are hit with a blunt object, had grown all around my heart; the largest one was attached to my aorta.

I later learned that the surgeons had cracked open my chest and used suction to remove the hematomas from my heart.

Part of my aorta and its valve were later replaced.

Still intubated, I stared at the ceiling and felt the warm sensation of tears rolling down my face. "Thank you Lord. I finally get it."

I looked at the beautiful faces of my family whom I had seen not in years and felt the pain that they tried so hard to hide with their smiles.

I finally get it. I pinched and moved each part of my body then thanked God for touching me with his Mercy and Grace. "Lord, I finally get it."

I get the fact that it ain't about me. Many a night I sat in my room feeling sorry for myself, but it ain't about me. It wasn't about me the times I was robbed and escaped injury and loss. It wasn't about me the dozens of times I placed myself in harms way and God made harm take a hard left turn.

The fact that my heart still diligently beats in my chest is proof enough to me that God is not finished with me yet.

As I laid on what easily could have my death bed, I knew then that God had a plan for my life. And it doesn't matter how hard I try to screw it up, God's will, will be done in my life and there is absolutely nothing that I can do about it.

I could not even kill myself to prevent it from happening.

While there in the intensive care ward, I befriended a man whose name was Ben. Ben had been hit by a car while walking in a cross walk and doctors thought that he would never walk again.

Ben was bitter and depressed about his situation and the hand that life had dealt him. He felt that though he had done nothing wrong he was to live his life with this handicap.

One day while Ben sat wallowing in his self created pool of self pity, a middle aged woman wearing a beige colored rain coat and brown pants walked into the room. The woman approached Ben's hospital bed apprehensively.

"I'm so glad to see that you are doing so well in your recovery. I have not been able to sleep since the accident." She told him.

"I'm sorry, do I know you", said Ben.

"No you don't. I was driving the car that hit you. I am so sorry." There was a long silence. "I monitored you progress while you were in your coma. I came by today to ask your forgiveness."

The woman eyes welled up and the tears streamed down her face.

During the ensuing silence, I witnessed emotional expressions that ranged from anger to forgiveness on Ben's face.

Ben then said, "It is within me to remain angry with you for the way you have changed my life. But that anger will do me no good. It will just make me a sad and bitter person. So I forgive you; not for your sake, but for mine."

Ben later told me that it was after that moment of acceptance that he felt that he was able to move on with his life.

It was then that I realized that the last thirteen years of my life had been a car wreck and that I am forced to live with the handicap of being a recovering addict for the rest of my life. That's the hand that life had dealt me.

The difference between my story and Ben's story is the fact that I was driving the car that hit me. "I", the victim, needed to forgive "me", the driver, for "me", the addict, to move on.

I forgave myself for neglecting my family for so many years. I forgave myself for disregarding my physical health and well being. I forgave myself for putting myself through years of physical and emotional abuse and suffering. I forgave myself for losing everything that I've ever owned and everyone in my life that cares about me. I forgave myself for the pain I have caused everyone in my life. I forgave myself for allowing my son to grow up without really knowing his father. I forgave myself for having to start my life over. I forgave myself for not including God in the mix.

Now that I have forgiven myself, I am free to move on.

Today, I'm no longer on a dope run. I'm now on a hope run. I chase hope with the same vigor, enthusiasm and determination that I utilized at another time in my life to chase dope.

On those days that I feel my energy waning, I remember the many times when I was exhausted from being awake for days. I rested not, but found the energy to engage my hustle because my addict was in need.

If I had used this philosophy over the course of my addiction, I would have been a very rich man many years ago.

But today I refuse to look back. I realize today that it's much too difficult to go forward while looking in the rear view mirror.

I'm no longer a hopeless dope fiend. I am a dopeless hope fiend.

MAKE MIRACLES

HAPPEN

There was once a baby eagle whose name was Ben. Ben had fallen from his nest and was adopted and raised by chickens.

Since Ben had no recollection of being an eagle, he felt content with living the life of a chicken. He would peck grain from the ground with his sister chicks and he never had the opportunity to soar like other eagles. He thought that he was a chicken.

One day the young eagle looked up and saw the glorious site of four adult eagles gracefully soaring among the clouds. Ben was impressed with their strength and stamina. Ben wanted so much to be like the eagles but had no hope of ever accomplishing this goal because, Of course, chickens can't fly.

After landing, one of the eagles walked over to Ben and said, "My young friend, you are more than you have become. You are living a lie; you have convinced yourself that your lot in life is merely to peck the ground for sustenance.

You were born to soar with the eagles. You are a master of your environment; instead you have become a victim of it. It's time for you to relinquish the ways of your peers and claim your place on the throne of nature.

We, as addicts, for too long have been living the life of Ben. I propose that we are more than we have become.

It is time for us to lift our heads from the ground and look upwards and imagine soaring like the eagles.

Because of our environment, we have convinced ourselves that we cannot achieve excellence in any area of our lives, and that our only lot is to toil in failure and mediocrity.

Ben had the same body, wingspan and genetics as those eagles that soared above. Nonetheless, the crucial difference between Ben and the ascending ones involved his thinking. His actions were totally based in his beliefs!

In order for us to be successful we must reprogram ourselves. We must change our way of thinking.

In society, drug addicts and alcoholics are seen as the scum of the earth. We are known for contributing nothing, but consuming much. We have no political prowess because we don't vote and we are flagged with the distinction of being law breakers and convicts.

We have been fed this garbage so much and for so long that its not surprising that we tend to believe it.

We have become comfortable living the life of the chicken.

But now that we are no longer under the oppressive weight of our addiction, we understand that we are not bad, getting good. We are sick, getting better.

And as we become better we also become wiser. We recognize that the gifts that are offered by life are within our grasp. And we waste no time claiming what is ours.

We do not turn our backs on our experiences. Our experiences are who we are. We use them as a means of improving our environment while being careful not to go back to the old ways.

There is no limit to what we can do if only we spread our wings and soar like an eagle.

We do not live in shame and disgrace for we have long forgiven ourselves for those misdeeds. We move forward never looking back.

We are uniquely qualified to face life's challenges head on. Compared to the problems that we have endured, the things that everyday people go through seem small.

Normal folk just have to deal with things such as paying bills, feeding the kids and other life issues.

At one time in our lives, we had to deal with all of those things plus the inconvenience of having a monster on our backs that tried to suck the life force out of us.

Since we overcame that, we realized that there is little that we can't accomplish.

Always remember that the world is ours for the taking.

I sometimes think of all the times that I tried to fix me. How vane of me to think that I could do such a thing. All I can do is admit that I am powerless and give it to God to handle.

This relieves me of a great burden. I don't have to worry about determining if I'm going to get better anymore. It's not my problem.

I felt like the weight of the world had been removed from my shoulders. I don't have to worry whether or not I was going to fail because I serve a God that can do anything, but fail.

It was then that I also really got the fact that my addiction to crack was only a symptom of my true disease of addiction.

I AM A RECOVERING ADDICT. MY PROBLEM IS MIKE

Above is how I introduce myself at 12 step meetings. When I say that, it reminds me that crack is not the problem. It's only the symptom. The problem is Mike and Mike's way of thinking.

No drug has ever jumped off the table and forced its way into my body without Mikes help.

As long as I work to improve Mike and focus not so much on the addiction to crack, there is a good chance that everything will be OK. One day at a time.

I had spent years being angry at myself and resenting myself. It's now time for me to forgive myself and love myself.

I HAVE TO KEEP REMINDING MYSELF THAT I'M NOT BAD, GETTING GOOD. I'M SICK, GETTING BETTER.

I have committed my life to helping others and in doing so, I help myself. Helping other addicts keeps me sober. Ralph, I finally get it.

I wake up everyday and thank God for giving me another day to do his will. Then I ask him to give me the strength to make it through another day without even the desire to use. I've been doing this everyday and everyday the answer to that prayer has been" yes".

I know this because I have not used today. Or yesterday. Or for many many days before yesterday. It is now 4:36 PM and I have not put any mind and mood altering substances in my body all day. Today is a good day.

THE BEGINNING !

IN LOVING MEMORY OF

MY FRIEND RALPH R.

A MAN WITH A HEART OF GOLD.

R.I.P.

38719136R00124

Made in the USA
Lexington, KY
21 January 2015